UNDERGROUND TRAIN FILE

SURFACE STOCK 1933–1959

Brian Hardy

Capital Transport

AUTHOR'S NOTE AND INTRODUCTION

This handbook covers the period from 1933 to 1959 and contains complete listings of all London Transport Surface Stock passenger rail vehicles in stock during that period and gives a description of each type.

Vehicles which were new during the period under review, and similarly those which were withdrawn and scrapped, are noted with the relevant dates alongside the appropriate cars. Previous numbers and cars involved in renumbering and conversions are also included. Quite often, the dates quoted will be 'official' dates, which may often be at variance with what actually happened – in some cases the dates may be a 'week-ending', or just a month and year – treat them with caution!

Prior to 1933, transport in London had been operated by a number of different companies and the new LPTB embraced those who operated Underground railways, buses and trams. Insofar as the Underground was concerned, it was a case of the Metropolitan Railway joining up with what had become the Underground Electric Railways of London (UERL), which comprised what we now know as the District, Bakerloo, Central, Piccadilly and Northern lines. The Metropolitan Railway (which included the Great Northern & City Railway) resisted being incorporated in the new LPTB right up to the end and even now some regard it as being the 'elite' of the Underground network.

The story then takes us through the Second World War. Some new rolling stock was being delivered but many of the older cars, which would normally have been scrapped, were kept as spare vehicles.

After the Second World War, there was much re-appraisal of the pre-war plans, which had a significant effect on rolling stock. The austere post-war conditions meant that any proposed new rolling stock came under intensive scrutiny and it would not be wrong to say that the R stock had a rather difficult birth! On the Metropolitan Line the electrification to Amersham was deferred as were many other projects that affected stations and infrastructure.

The date of 1959 was chosen for the end date for a number of reasons. Experiments had taken place on the District Line with unpainted aluminium trains. In 1955 there was just one train, but the all-silver look was just around the corner – by 1959 large orders had been placed for unpainted aluminium rolling stock for both 'surface' and 'tube' lines and a third batch of R stock also comprised unpainted vehicles.

This publication would not have been possible without the kind help of Dr Andrew Gilks, who spent many hours meticulously recording the disposal details of the older rolling stock types, Fred Ivey, J. Graeme Bruce OBE, who was involved with LT rolling stock for all of his working life, and to Piers Connor for his immaculate records on London Transport railway rolling stock. And, of course, to London Transport, whose decision to run down the Car Records office at Acton Works in the late-1970s enabled the rescue of many historical records and data, which would otherwise have been consigned to the dustbin. My thanks also go to my wife Jeanne, for her help with the typescript and checking of the numerical data.

CONTENTS

Front cover Most of the R stock was painted in red livery but one complete eight-car unpainted train entered service in January 1953. Initially it had the red waist band straight across the front but, because it cut into the train set number box, it was altered within a few weeks to form a 'V' shape. *LT Museum*

Title page When the single G class cars were unavailable for the South Acton shuttle, a two-coach crew-operated set of Q stock substituted, such as 4193 and 4148 seen at Acton Town. *Photomatic*

First published 2002
ISBN 185414 247 X
Published by Capital Transport Publishing, 38 Long Elmes, Harrow Weald, Middlesex
Printed by CS Graphics, Singapore

CHAPTER ONE

THE METROPOLITAN RAILWAY SALOON STOCK

The story of the Metropolitan Railway's 'Saloon' stock is very complex. It comprises three different batches built in 1904–06 for the Uxbridge line and Inner Circle, similar cars that were built in 1906 for the Hammersmith & City Line (that were jointly owned by the Great Western Railway), subsequent batches for the Metropolitan (in 1913–14 and 1920–21), along with the cars on the Great Northern & City Railway, which passed to 'Metropolitan' ownership in 1913. There were also three odd cars, which had been built for experimental purposes. For this reason, only a summary of the stocks can be attempted here.

Until the first of the electric stock was built, the Metropolitan Railway had numbered its vehicles in sequence from '1' upwards, irrespective of the type of car. This continued with all compartment type stock, with minor exceptions, right up to the early 1930s. With the electric saloon stock, however, each car type began at '1', so in each train, there could be two or three vehicles bearing the same numbers. The various batches of cars as built were as follows:

The front half of a Metropolitan Railway first class driving trailer (as the 'Met' preferred to call them) at Watford, having recently been renumbered 6505 by London Transport. This is a 1904-built car, a feature being the narrow car windows. *D.W.K. Jones*

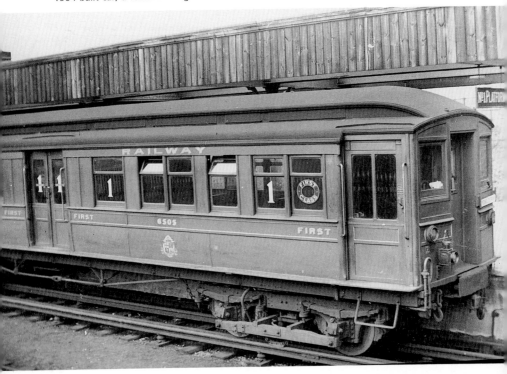

DRIVING MOTOR CARS

1–20	*	1904	20
21–56	†	1905	36
57–82		1906	26
83–105	§	1913–14	23
106–125	§	1921	20
126–165		1906	H&C	40
166–197		1904–06	GN&C	32
198–199	§	1926	2 **199 cars**

1ST CLASS DRIVING TRAILERS

1–20		1904	20
21–56	†	1905	36
57–76	†	1906	20
77–86	§	1913–14	10
87–92	§	1921	6
93–105		1904–06	GN&C	13
106	§	1924	1 **106 cars**

3RD CLASS TRAILERS

1–30		1904	30
31–56		1905	26
57–76	†	1906	20
77–86	§	1913–14	10
87–119	§	1921	33
120–159		1906	H&C	40
160–190		1904–06	GN&C	31
191–208	†	1904–05	Ex-motor cars from series 2–55 converted 1929–31	– **190 cars**

COMPOSITE TRAILERS

1–7	†	1905–06	Ex–1DTs series 21–76	–
8–10	†	1906	Ex–3T series 51–76	–
11–50		1906	H&C	40 **40 cars**
GRAND TOTAL:				**535 cars**

Notes:

* Original No.18 motor coach replaced by new car in 1906.

§ Elliptical-roofed stock – all others clerestory roofs.

† Composite trailers 1–7 were ex-1DTs 29, 33, 50, 71–74. Composite trailers 8–10 were ex-3Ts 65, 69, 71. Trailers 191–208 were ex-motor cars 2, 13, 21, 26, 28, 39, 36, 44, 10, 4, 49, 45, 1, 27, 15, 12, 48, 55 respectively.

It will be seen from the above table that many conversions within the saloon stock fleet took place before acquisition by the London Passenger Transport Board. Ten composite trailers were provided for the newly electrified East London Line service in 1913, because this line operated shorter train lengths that the others, while in 1929–31 a total of 18 motor coaches were converted to trailers. Prior to all this, driving motor car No.18 of 1904 vintage was retained by British Westinghouse to demonstrate their single-phase system. A new car was offered as a replacement and was built identical to the second batch in 1906, including enclosed vestibules.

The original rolling stock order was for ten seven-car trains, although the 50 trailer cars were ordered six months before the motors, because the electrical equipment to be used was then undecided. Built by Metropolitan Amalgamated in 1904 the cars were 52ft 6ins long and 8ft 9ins wide. All had clerestory roofs, as did most other contemporary rolling stock of that era. A second batch of trains followed in 1905 and comprised 18 six-car trains. In fact, the order for trailer cars

Interior of a 1904 Metropolitan first class driving trailer in May 1934 in the early days of the LPTB. The narrow saloon windows of the 1904 cars is evident. Note the elaborate finish to the car ceiling and interior fittings. *LT Museum*

was reduced by ten, because the same number of trailers from the 1904 batch were available, and the inadequate platform lengths prevented the operation of seven-car trains that was originally proposed. Whilst similar in appearance, the 1905 cars were distinguishable by having wider saloon windows. This difference was continued on a third batch in 1906, which gave a fleet total of 38 six-car trains, with six motor cars as spares. All motor cars had a luggage compartment behind an enclosed driver's cab, while the passenger access on the 1904 cars was through gates at the car ends. This proved an unsuitable arrangement for outdoor operation and the end gates were later replaced with enclosed ends with hand-operated sliding doors. The 1905 and subsequent stocks were delivered with enclosed ends. Despite this, the passenger access to the cars via end doors was unsatisfactory and a programme commenced in 1911 to fit centre doors to improve station stop times. Because this work was extensive and time-consuming, various trials were undertaken. The reduction in seating was generally ten in motor cars (from 48 to 38) and eight in trailers (56 to 48), but there were differences.

Although the Uxbridge line opened on 4 July 1904 it was not until 1 January 1905 that the electric trains were introduced, a changeover process that continued until mid-March 1905. The Inner Circle began electric operation on 1 July 1905 but was hastily withdrawn on the same day because of problems with the shoegear on the new trains, which overturned current rails on District Railway metals. The Metropolitan's equipment was slightly different to that on the District (whose tracks the former shared between South Kensington and Minories Junction), where the shoes were mounted outside the bogie frame. The District Railway had their current collector shoes mounted on a shoebeam between the bogie's axleboxes and thus all Metropolitan stock was withdrawn for modification. Electric services were resumed on the Inner Circle on 13 September 1905, being completed by 24 September 1905. Traffic levels on the Inner Circle did not reached anticipated numbers and train lengths were reduced to four cars, giving a surplus of trailers.

A three-car train of Hammersmith & City stock, built in 1906, stands in the northern bay road at Kensington – Addison Road on 26 August 1933, just over after a month after the stock was absorbed by London Transport. The cars have yet to receive their new numbers. On the left is driving trailer 156 (which became 6261) and adjacent trailer 47 (which later became 9257). This shuttle service to and from Edgware Road was withdrawn in 1940 and not reinstated. *H.C. Casserley*

Metropolitan Amalgamated also built 20x6-car trains for the electrification of the Hammersmith & City Line in 1906. They were broadly similar in appearance to their 1905–06 counterparts of the Metropolitan, having wide saloon windows and motor cars with luggage compartments, but initially had destination indicators over the cab front. The driving cab windows were not so deep. In common with Metropolitan Railway practice, each type of car was again numbered upwards from '1'.

The Hammersmith & City stock was jointly owned by the Metropolitan and Great Western, although the former undertook all maintenance at Hammersmith depot. Each car had "Great Western & Metropolitan Railways" on one side of the car, with "Metropolitan & Great Western Railways" on the other.

The composite trailers were located in the middle of trains but in 1908–09 they were converted to driving trailers to enable short trains to be operated in off-peak times. The necessity to standardise the position of first class cars led to the composite control trailers being converted to 3rd class and the third class trailers to composites around the same time, because hitherto, the shorter formation of Circle Line trains meant that the first class car would not always be in the same position.

The Hammersmith & City stock was similarly converted to have centre doors but this was done after the Metropolitan's own stock, between 1918 and 1921. The H&C stock was renumbered by the Metropolitan Railway in 1925, following on from like numbered cars of that company. Motor cars 1–40 thus became 126–165, third class driving trailers 1–40 became 120–159, while composite trailers 1–40 became 11–50.

The independent Great Northern & City Railway chose to have its current rails mounted outside the running rails. Its rolling stock was built in two batches. The first was ordered in 1902 and was ready when the line opened on 14 February 1904. This comprised 26 motor cars and 32 trailers, all with wooden bodies. The

Electric Railway & Tramway Carriage Works at Preston built six seven-car trains (18 motors and 24 trailers) and Brush of Loughborough built the remaining 16 cars (eight motors and eight trailers). The cars were numbered 10–35 (motors) and 40–71 (trailers).

The apparent illogical decision to begin the number series at '10' is explained by the fact that the GN&C was originally planned to have hauled through GNR trains to Moorgate, for which nine electric locomotives were proposed. Only one (No.1) was ever built which was confined to shunting duties in Drayton Park depot. This left a gap in the numbering sequence, so that the line's electric passenger stock therefore began at '10'. After the line had opened, additional stock was ordered from Brush, comprising five motor cars and 13 trailers, all of which were built with steel bodies. The trailers were simply numbered at the end of the sequence (72–84) but four of the five motor cars were numbered 35–39 (in the space available) with the fifth becoming No.9 in the space at the very beginning. The additional cars were delivered from late-1905 and into 1906.

All cars had end and centre doors, although the latter were used only at terminal stations. Seating capacity was 54 (wooden motor cars), 58 (wooden trailers), 60 (steel motor cars) and 64 (steel trailers).

Within the first three years of service, the GN&C made a number of alterations to its rolling stock. Plans to run seven-car trains with three motor cars (one being in the middle) were abandoned probably before opening and a desire to operate short trains in slack hours saw 12 trailers converted into control trailers. The driving equipment for these came from the wooden-bodied motor cars (these were delivered 'double-ended') and they also provided the driving equipment for the new steel motor cars built by Brush. Very few, if any, wooden motor cars actually survived in double-ended form. A fatal staff accident involving motor car No.13 resulted in this car being renumbered to 8, while in 1907, steel trailer car 84 was converted to a motor car and renumbered 7. The GN&C stock then comprised 32 motor cars (26 wooden and 6 steel), 12 control trailers (all wooden-bodied) and 32 trailers (20 wooden and 12 steel).

For financial reasons the Metropolitan Railway took control of the GN&C from 30 June 1913. It set about improving its 'main line' status by providing first class accommodation on trains, which began on 15 February 1915. To that end, 13 wooden trailers were converted to have first class accommodation which resulted in more spacious seating arrangements (but with four less seats per car). Renumbering of the stock took place from 1923 and the GN&C cars, suitably renumbered, were added to the end of the Metropolitan's own stock. Motor cars became 166–197, third class trailers and control trailers 160–190 and first class trailers 93–105.

Two main factors were the reason behind the Metropolitan Railway ordering additional stock for delivery in 1913 from MCW&F. This was the electrification of the East London Line and the reconstruction of Baker Street station, the latter enabling more trains to work through to the City. The order comprised 23 motor coaches, ten first class driving trailers and ten third class trailers. The tradition of providing a luggage compartment behind the driver's cab on motor cars was continued but centre sliding doors were provided from new, as well as end single sliding doors. The most noticeable difference was the abandonment of clerestory car roofs in favour of elliptical roofs. Motor cars were numbered 83–105, first class driving trailers 77–86 and third class trailers similarly 77–86. At this time also, to provide composite trailers for the East London Line service, ten existing cars were so converted, seven ex-first class and three ex-third class.

A total of 16 motor cars of the 1913 stock were rebuilt after the First World War, by removing the luggage compartment, thereby increasing seating capacity from 38 to 46. The luggage side doors were sealed but no windows replaced them, indicating perhaps the urgency of additional passenger accommodation. This was

A 1913-built motor car leads a five-car train of Metropolitan Railway 'saloon' stock into Moorgate *c.*1948, being one of 18 trains specially refurbished for this service in the mid-1930s. By this time, the red and cream livery had given way to all-red. It should be noted that the 1913 cars had centre double doors and end single doors. The space immediately behind the driving cab was originally the luggage compartment. *Author's collection*

Interior of a 1913-built Metropolitan Railway saloon stock motor car, all of which were built with elliptical roofs. In this March 1934 view, the ceiling is more simply finished than the older cars. *LT Museum*

only a stop-gap measure, for increases in traffic required more trains. Because the Metropolitan operated both saloon and compartment stocks, opinions varied as to which offered the better facilities for passengers. Unsatisfactory experience with saloon cars without centre doors led to a six-car train being rebuilt by MCW&F in 1919, comprising motor cars numbered 36 and 44, first class trailers 53 and 55, and third class trailers 35 and 67. The new arrangement saw outward-opening hinged doors provided along the car (five per side on trailers, four on motors), which gave access to vestibules, either side of which were pairs of facing transverse seats protected by draught screens. The main exterior change was that the clerestory roofs had been replaced by elliptical roofs. The rebuilt set was called the 'Hustle' train but it was not as successful as hoped and in the end, additional saloon stock cars – the 1921 stock – were ordered instead. This comprised 20 motor cars (106–125), six first class control trailers (87–92) and 33 third class trailers (87–119). They were similar in appearance to the 1913 stock but had three pairs of double sliding doors per car side and no end single doors. Motor cars had the traditional luggage compartment and seated 37, first class trailers 45 and third class trailers 50. This stock enabled service improvements on the Metropolitan Line and the increase of Circle Line trains from four cars back to five cars.

Mention should also be made of three other cars, all of which had saloon interiors. The first was a driving trailer built in 1923 similar to the 1921 stock, and was exhibited at the Empire Exhibition at Wembley in 1924/25 before entering service.

Metropolitan Railway 'saloon' stock built in 1920/21 had three pairs of double doors but no end single doors as seen on this Circle Line train at South Kensington. *F.G. Reynolds*

The unique three-coach set of 1923–26 saloon stock ended its days on the East London Line, being scrapped in the early-1950s along with the Circle stock. *John H. Meredith*

It was numbered 106. The other two cars were motor coaches ordered in 1925 and were built by Metro Carriage. Additional stock for the Metropolitan's Watford extension was required and these two motor cars (198–199) were the prototypes, having Metropolitan Vickers equipment. They were similar to the 1921 motor cars but immediately behind the driver was an above-floor equipment compartment, behind which was the traditional luggage area with the passenger saloon behind that – seating was reduced in consequence. Whilst the equipment performed adequately and orders were placed for more trains, Metropolitan Railway passengers in Hertfordshire preferred compartment stock, so the two prototype saloon cars remained unique. When the motor cars of the 'Hustle' train were converted to trailers in 1929–31, giving six trailers in all of this type, motor cars 198 and 199 operated with them, forming an eight-coach train. In latter days, the two motor cars and the 1923 control trailer worked together as a three-car set, relegated to the East London Line shuttle service.

The Metropolitan's saloon stock therefore numbered 535 cars. A total of 522 were inherited by the LPTB on 1 July 1933, with the deficiency of 13 accounted for as follows:

- Severely-damaged motor cars 46 and 69 converted into double-ended compartment cars for the Metropolitan shuttle services in 1910 – see also page 100.
- Ten first class control trailers converted to compartment 'Dreadnoughts'.
- First class control trailer 66 converted to a surface stock gauging car in 1934.

All 13 cars were taken over by the LPTB in their subsequent guises. In addition, 18 motor cars from the 1904–05 batches had been converted to trailers in 1929–31.

A numbering scheme was drawn up in 1930 by the Underground Group, where individual groups of cars were given blocks of numbers according to their type. The LPTB continued with the programme and also applied it to the ex-Metropolitan Line saloon stock, for which 'convenient' gaps had been left, 2xxx for motor cars, 6xxx for driving trailers (which became 'control trailers' in London Transport parlance) and 9xxx for trailers. These were further sub-divided as follows:

22xx	62xx	92xx	Hammersmith & City
25xx	65xx	94xx and 95xx	Main line stock
29xx	69xx	99xx	Great Northern & City

The 522 cars therefore were given the following numbers, although not all were numbered in sequence and not all numbers were utilised.

DRIVING MOTOR CARS

2200–2207	1905–06	8		Main Line stock on H&C
2208–2247	1906	40		H&C stock
2500–2545	1904–06	46		2500–2505 on GN&C from 1930 – not renumbered in GN&C series
2546–2552	1914	7		
2553–2560	1905	8		
2561–2580	1921	20		
2581–2596	1913–14	16		
2598–2599	1926	2		
2900–2940	1902–06	32		GN&C stock **179 cars**

DRIVING TRAILERS

6201–6203	1905–06	2	1st		
6211–6212	1905–06	2	1/3	} Main Line stock on H&C	
6220–6224	1905–06	5	3rd		
6225–6264	1906	40	3rd	H&C stock	
6500–6538	1904–06	39	1st		
6539–6541	1921	3	1st		
6542–6550	1913	9	1st		
6551–6553	1921	3	1st		
6554–6556	1905	3	1st		
6557	1926	1	1st		
6580–6587	1905–06	8	1/3		
6590–6598	1906	9	3rd		
6900–6919	1902–06	12	3rd	GN&C stock	**136 cars**

TRAILERS

9200–9203	1905–06	4	1st	Main Line stock on H&C	
9210–9212	1905–06	3	3rd	Main Line stock on H&C	
9220–9259	1906	40	1/3	H&C stock	
9400–9410	1905–06	11	1st		
9483–9538	1904–06	56	3rd		
9539–9548	1913	10	3rd		
9549–9581	1921	33	3rd		
9582–9599	1904–05	18	3rd	Ex-motor cars	
9900–9912	1902–06	13	1st	GN&C stock	
9950–9968	1902–06	19	3rd	GN&C stock	**207 cars**

GRAND TOTAL: **522 cars**

In its early days, London Transport set about sorting out a very diverse and complex fleet of vehicles. This comprised:

- The scrapping of surplus cars in 1935–36 from the main line fleet and the GN&C.
- A total of 15 cars renumbered in 1935–36. A pair of motor cars (2530 and 2535) exchanged numbers, while an interchange between trailers and control trailers and the class of accommodation provided also took place.
- Six motor cars of 1905 vintage were experimentally fitted with Metadyne equipment. These were repainted in LT red and cream livery.
- The provision of a dedicated fleet of renovated trains for the Inner Circle service.

The Metropolitan referred to its saloon stock as V and VT stock. The V stock comprised all-vestibuled cars, while the VT stock comprised vestibuled trailers with compartment stock motors.

Below The Great Northern & City Line's depot at Drayton Park was a very cramped site, where a six-car train is seen on the ramp leading to the depot sheds. Nearest the camera is an original wooden motor coach. Note the unique current rail arrangement on this line, which lasted until tube stock took over in May 1939. *Author's collection*

Bottom No.69, one of the two Metropolitan Railway compartment shuttle coaches that were converted from 'saloon' stock following accident damage, is seen leaving Stanmore for Wembley Park on 5 August 1934, before renumbering by the LPTB to 2769. *LCGB/Ken Nunn collection*

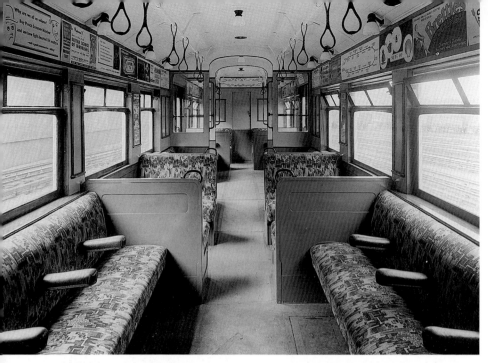

One of the tasks undertaken by the new LPTB was the renovation of selected cars of Metropolitan 'saloon' stock, to create a dedicated fleet for the Circle Line service. This included installing end communicating doors, LT-type light fittings and seating with leather armrests. *LT Museum*

The Circle Line project involved 90 cars, to form 18x5-car trains, with 14x5 for service (seven trains per 'Circle') and 4x5-car trains spare. The renovation work began in 1934, the first entering service on 8 March, and enabled the cars to continue in service until the end of 1950, although their replacement began in 1947. The remainder of the fleet, apart from three other cars, were withdrawn in the early years of the Second World War. The 90 cars comprised 36 motor cars, 18 control trailers and 36 trailers. The control trailers, although not being used for uncoupling purposes, were required in each train formation for their first class accommodation.

All 59 cars of 1921 stock were selected for renovation but the total number of these cars available fell short of the total required. Thus, 16 DMs, eight control trailers and three trailers of 1913 stock were also renovated. Four 1905 control trailers made up the shortfall of this type of car and initially were the only clerestory-roofed cars in the 'Circle' fleet. Modifications included the removal of the driving equipment from the control trailers, removal of the luggage compartments on motor cars, fitting communicating doors in all car ends and 13 motor cars converted to single equipments. The Circle fleet in fact comprised five trains with BTH200 equipment and 13 trains with BWE200 equipment. The traction motors on the latter were unsatisfactory and the opportunity was taken to replace them by motors available from scrapped District stock. These were found to be over-powerful, and 13 motor cars were reduced to single equipments, being 2561–2562, 2573–2580 and 2584–2586. Each of these 13 five-car trains therefore had six motors instead of eight.

Inside the cars, the seats were reupholstered and LT type light fittings installed. But perhaps the most noticeable difference was the exterior repainting in LT red and cream livery (which later gave way to all red).

Two changes were made to the Circle Line fleet after renovation. The first was as a result of a collision at Charing Cross on 17 May 1938, where motor car 2564 was damaged beyond repair. Its place was taken by 1913 car 2552, whose number was retained, although it acquired the bogies and equipment from 2564. On 9 March 1941, motor car 2589 was damaged beyond repair by enemy action at King's Cross. Because most other saloon stock had either been scrapped or spoken for in other uses (q.v. below), the body of 1905 motor car 2558 replaced it, but this was renumbered 2589 and was the only 'Circle' motor car with a clerestory roof.

As previously mentioned, the withdrawal of surplus saloon stock began in 1935, but wholesale withdrawal did not begin until 1938 (Hammersmith & City stock – replaced by new O stock), 1939 (GN&C stock – superseded by displaced Pre-1938 Tube Stock) and 1939–41 (main line stock – displaced by new P stock). All this was as a result of the 1935–40 New Works Programme, but the outbreak of the Second World War on 3 September 1939 had a profound effect on much of the saloon stock that remained. Initially, 12x6-cars of Hammersmith & City stock and 12x6 cars of Metropolitan stock were to be kept but this plan was subsequently changed and many other cars found other uses. The GN&C rolling stock, displaced by May 1939, was scrapped quite quickly, because that line had operated a unique outside current rail system until then. For many other cars, it was a different story.

A number of withdrawn cars were stored in various sidings, which included Willesden Green, Ealing Common (the 'alps' depot sidings) and Acton Town. The sidings at Acton Town were laid temporarily just east of the station on the east side of the South Acton branch. Cars already deemed as 'scrapped' were located on LT property and had various uses. These included:

- Control trailer 6529 served as a car examiner's hut in Uxbridge sidings. This was an odd car that remained 'on the books' until scrapped in 1954.

- Trailer 9489 was 'scrapped' in 1941 but was used by the Home Guard in Hillingdon goods yard, being finally disposed of in 1946.

- Control trailers 6235, 6525 and 6587, listed as 'scrapped' in 1941, were used at Acton as rifle ranges in camouflaged condition.

The odd-man-out in the Circle fleet was DM 2589, which had replaced a car destroyed at King's Cross in 1941. It was the only Circle Line motor car with a clerestory roof, the body being acquired from withdrawn car 2552. Behind the 1906 motor car is a 1921 trailer, followed by a 1913 driving trailer, a 1921 trailer and a 1913 motor. *F.G. Reynolds*

By far the largest number of cars were either put to use elsewhere after disposal, or sold directly from London Transport. Examples of the former included:

- Hammersmith & City cars 9210 and 6233 were at Neasden (LNER) engine shed.
- An unidentified coach was used for training Civil Defence personnel in Crystal Palace Park.

Under the latter circumstances, a total of 171 cars were put to further uses between 1940 and 1944, the disposal dates from London Transport being listed with the individual cars at the end.

Officers Quarters for the Admiralty –

6500   6502   6581

Home Guard use –

6525 9489 9497 9522

Tank Target Units –

2202 2213 2221 2225 2235 2240 2242 2246 2538

MOD Shoeburyness

6503 9410 9480 9486 9538

Personnel Car for the Admiralty, Newhaven –

6511 6583

For the Admiralty at Weymouth (HMS Bee) –

9524 9540 9585

Converted for Ministry of Fuel –

Sleeping Cars:	6222 (020007)	6509 (020004)	9492 (020001)
	9513 (020003)	9594 (020002)	
Dining Cars:	6517 (020009)	6526 (020010)	
Kitchen Cars:	6519 (020006)	6520 (020008)	
Staff Car:	9529 (020005)		

Cars to Southern Command as Hutments –

6234 6250 6506 6508 6531 6532 6554 6556 6560 6561 6586 6590
9212 9481 9483 9485 9502 9503 9504 9506 9507 9511 9514 9519
9528 9533 9535 9536 9582 9584 9590 9593 9597

Car bodies to Southern Command –

2208 2209 2214 2217 2218 2219 2220 2231 2238 2247 2546 2547
2548 2549 2550 2551 6212 6223 6230 6231 6237 6240 6243 6244
6248 6249 6251 6253 6256 6262 6264 6501 6505 6507 6513 6514
6515 6524 6528 6530 6535 6555 6558 6580 6592 6598 9203 9211
9226 9238 9239 9250 9252 9258 9479 9484 9487 9490 9491 9493
9494 9495 9496 9498 9501 9508 9512 9516 9517 9521 9523 9526
9530 9531 9586 9588 9589 9596

Further service of a more dignified form befell four six-car trains of mostly Hammersmith & City stock. To maintain transport links under the River Mersey should any rolling stock become damaged, four trains were converted for use on the Liverpool Central – Rock Ferry, New Brighton and West Kirby routes. This was actually one of three options, the others being to use LMS electric stock from the London area (and then using stored tube stock on those services) or to use

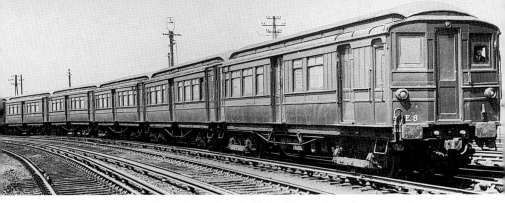

A six-car train of Hammersmith & City stock, probably in Birkenhead North depot yard. This was one of four trains loaned to the Mersey Railway during the Second World War as standby rolling stock, should any trains become damaged. In the event, it is believed that none ever carried passengers there, their only outings being for crew familiarisation. Driving motor car E8 (ex-2228) is nearest the camera. *Author's collection*

stored London tube stock in Liverpool, both of which were rejected, the former because the LMS London area electric stock was unsuitable for tunnel working, the latter because of the height differences between platforms and trains. Between November 1941 and February 1942 therefore, a total of 22 ex-Hammersmith & City cars and two Metropolitan cars, all with clerestory roofs, were converted and transferred to Liverpool. They were painted in LMS red. Driving motor cars were numbered E1–8, trailers E11–18 and control trailers E21–28, as follows:

Driving Motor Cars			Trailers			Driving Trailers		
E1	2233	E5	2239	E11	9228	E15	9231	E21	6238	E25	6211
E2	2230	E6	2537	E12	9259	E16	9222	E22	6203	E26	6582
E3	2200	E7	2207	E13	9224	E17	9255	E23	6255	E27	6259
E4	2227	E8	2228	E14	9241	E18	9220	E24	6241	E28	6254

It is thought that these four 'emergency' trains never carried passengers, their only outings being on crew familiarisation runs and for trips to keep them in serviceable condition – they were normally kept in sidings at Birkenhead North and Hoylake. After the end of hostilities the trains were scrapped.

The fate of the other cars which saw service in some form or another during the war is not known. Indeed it is possible that the lists above are incomplete – after all, such activities during the war were secret, so the lists may only be regarded as complete insofar as information is available.

The ten cars converted for the Ministry of Fuel survived for a few more years until scrapped during the 1950s but it is quite likely that after the war, the majority of others were soon disposed of. A small few survived in private hands for a little longer as garden sheds, chicken runs, etc.

Meanwhile, the few saloon stock cars that remained out of service but still on London Transport's books were scrapped – 18 in 1945, seven in 1948 and one in 1954. No other changes took place to the Circle Line's 90 cars, apart from those previously mentioned. Their replacement began in February 1947, using five-car trains of P stock with Metadyne equipment. This process was rather slow, however, because of early post-war material shortages which had a detrimental effect on London Transport's desire to build new trains and convert others. It was not until 31 December 1950 that the last of the old Circle stock ran in passenger service, with disposals not beginning until October 1950. In addition to the 90 cars disposed of at the same time were the three odd cars of 1923–26 vintage (2598, 2599 and 6557) that survived as a three-car oddity on the East London Line, working alongside the District's handworked door stock.

In the lists that follow, the LT numbers are shown as first allocated by the LPTB. Subsequent renumberings are shown in the same lists to reduce confusion. The final LT number is shown in bold.

'MAIN LINE' STOCK DRIVING MOTOR COACHES – 99

Met. No.	Built	LT No.	Reno.	Date	Disposal	Met No.	Built	LT No.	Reno.	Date	Disposal
30	1905	2500 §			26.09.38	103	1913	2550			07.01.41
32	1905	2501 §			26.04.39	104	1913	2551			04.01.41
31	1905	2502 §			26.04.39	105	1913	2552 C			27.03.51
34	1905	2503 §			26.04.39	63	1906	2553			22.02.40
33	1905	2504 §			26.04.39	64	1906	2554			01.05.36
35	1905	2505 §			26.09.38	65	1906	2555			11.10.43
3	1904	2506			12.02.36	66	1906	2556			30.10.43
5	1904	2507			02.05.36	67	1906	2557			30.10.43
6	1904	2508			03.09.37	68	1906	2558 C	2589	28.06.41	11.12.50
7	1904	2509			03.03.36	70	1906	2559			30.10.43
8	1904	2510			18.03.36	77	1906	2560			08.05.46
9	1904	2511			05.02.36	106	1921	2561 C			09.10.50
11	1904	2512			12.02.36	107	1921	2562 C			08.01.51
14	1904	2513			18.03.36	116	1921	2563 C			20.11.50
16	1904	2514			03.09.37	117	1921	2564 C			22.06.39
17	1904	2515			12.02.36	118	1921	2565 C			20.11.50
18	1907	2516 #			29.06.36	119	1921	2566 C			11.12.50
19	1904	2517			12.02.36	120	1921	2567 C			14.03.51
20	1904	2518			29.06.36	121	1921	2568 C			14.02.51
22	1905	2519			05.02.36	122	1921	2569 C			30.10.50
23	1905	2520			05.02.36	123	1921	2570 C			20.02.51
24	1905	2521 ‡			15.06.37	124	1921	2571 C			23.10.50
25	1905	2522 ‡			15.06.37	125	1921	2572 C			07.11.50
28	1905	2523			03.09.37	108	1921	2573 C			08.01.51
37	1905	2524 ‡			15.06.37	109	1921	2574 C			05.03.51
38	1905	2525			17.02.38	110	1921	2575 C			27.11.50
40	1905	2526			05.02.36	111	1921	2576 C			27.11.50
41	1905	2527			18.03.36	112	1921	2577 C			14.02.51
42	1905	2528			18.03.36	113	1921	2578 C			14.03.51
43	1905	2529 ‡			15.06.37	114	1921	2579 C			20.02.51
47	1905	2530 ‡	2535	03.06.36	15.06.37	115	1921	2580 C			30.10.50
50	1905	2531			03.03.36	93	1913	2581 C			13.11.50
51	1905	2532			05.02.36	94	1913	2582 C			26.01.51
52	1905	2533			03.03.36	95	1913	2583 C			04.12.50
53	1905	2534			03.03.36	96	1913	2584 C			27.03.51
54	1905	2535 ‡	2530	03.06.36	15.03.37	97	1913	2585 C			09.10.50
56	1905	2536			02.05.36	98	1913	2586 C			23.10.50
72	1906	2537 †			21.11.45	83	1913	2587 C			05.03.51
75	1906	2538			01.09.42	84	1913	2588 C			22.12.50
78	1906	2539			02.11.45	85	1913	2589 C			02.05.41
57	1906	2540			03.03.42	86	1913	2590 C			13.11.50
58	1906	2541			30.10.43	87	1913	2591 C			04.12.50
59	1906	2542			02.11.45	88	1913	2592 C			15.01.51
60	1906	2543			30.10.43	89	1913	2593 C			07.11.50
61	1906	2544			30.10.43	90	1913	2594 C			26.02.51
62	1906	2545			24.03.41	91	1913	2595 C			15.01.51
99	1913	2546			10.01.41	92	1913	2596 C			26.02.51
100	1913	2547			07.01.41	198	1926	2598			16.04.51
101	1913	2548			04.01.41	199	1926	2599			16.04.51
102	1913	2549			07.01.41						

DRIVING TRAILERS – 75

Met. No.	Built	LT No.	Reno.	Date	Disposal	Met No.	Built	LT No.	Reno.	Date	Disposal
1	1904	6500			16.10.40	51	1905	6536 C			27.11.50
2	1904	6501			24.11.40	47	1905	6537 C			27.03.51
3	1904	6502			21.10.40	49	1905	6538 C			11.12.50
4	1904	6503			24.08.44	90	1921	6539 C			23.10.50
5	1904	6504			10.04.46	91	1921	6540 C			05.03.51
6	1904	6505			28.11.40	92	1921	6541 C			08.01.51
7	1904	6506			12.11.40	77	1913	6542	6533	25.07.35	10.04.46
8	1904	6507			20.12.40	79	1913	6543 C			15.01.51
9	1904	6508			26.08.40	80	1913	6544 C			14.02.51
10	1904	6509			12.10.43	81	1913	6545 C			09.10.50
11	1904	6510			28.07.45	82	1913	6546 C			26.02.51
12	1904	6511			01.05.43	83	1913	6547 C			20.02.51
13	1904	6512			28.07.45	84	1913	6548 C			30.10.50
14	1904	6513			24.02.41	85	1913	6549 C			13.11.50
15	1904	6514			24.11.40	86	1913	6550 C			07.11.50
16	1904	6515			28.11.40	87	1921	6551 C			16.04.51
17	1904	6516			02.11.45	88	1921	6552 C			16.04.51
18	1904	6517			12.10.43	89	1921	6553 C			20.11.50
19	1904	6518			08.05.46	54	1921	6554			26.08.40
20	1904	6519			12.10.43	55	1921	6555			27.02.41
21	1905	6520			12.10.43	56	1921	6556			12.11.40
23	1905	6521			21.06.41	106	1926	6557			04.12.50
24	1905	6522			10.04.46	29	1905	6580 *			07.02.41
25	1905	6523			18.07.45	33	1905	6581 *			21.10.40
27	1905	6524			28.11.40	50	1905	6582 *			† 22.11.45
31	1905	6525			30.08.41	71	1906	6583 *			01.05.43
32	1905	6526			12.10.43	74	1906	6584 *			18.07.45
35	1905	6527			08.05.46	65	1906	6585 *	6560	23.02.35	26.08.40
36	1905	6528			07.02.41	69	1906	6586 *			26.08.40
37	1905	6529			26.04.54	71	1906	6587 *			05.07.41
39	1905	6530			07.02.41	37	1906	6590			18.11.40
40	1905	6531			12.11.40	40	1906	6592			28.11.40
43	1905	6532			12.11.40	42	1906	6593			28.07.45
46	1905	6533 C	6542	27.07.35	09.10.50	47	1906	6596			02.11.45
52	1905	6534			22.04.48	49	1906	6598			02.12.40
53	1905	6535			27.02.41						

RENUMBERED FROM TRAILERS:

Met. No.	Built	LT No.	Reno.	Date	Disposal	Met No.	Built	LT No.	Reno.	Date	Disposal
59	1906	9402	6558	21.01.35	07.02.41	60	1906	9403	6561	02.03.35	18.11.40
70	1906	9408	6559	26.01.35	18.07.45	57	1906	9400	6562†	16.02.35	28.07.45

TRAILERS – 128

Met. No.	Built	LT No.	Reno.	Date	Disposal	Met. No.	Built	LT No.	Reno.	Date	Disposal
58	1906	9401			17.02.38	64	1906	9529			12.10.43
61	1906	9404	9477	12.01.35	08.05.46	66	1906	9530			06.12.40
63	1906	9405			29.06.36	67	1906	9531			24.02.41
64	1906	9406			27.07.36	68	1906	9532			18.07.45
65	1906	9407	9478	12.01.35	08.05.46	70	1906	9533			12.11.40
75	1906	9409			29.06.36	72	1906	9534			02.11.45
78	1912	9410			10.03.43	73	1906	9535			12.11.40
1	1904	9483			26.08.40	74	1906	9536			12.11.40
2	1904	9484			24.11.40	75	1906	9537			10.04.46
3	1904	9485			26.08.40	76	1906	9538			10.03.43
4	1904	9486			10.03.43	84	1913	9539			15.07.48
5	1904	9487			04.01.41	85	1913	9540			17.07.43
6	1904	9488			02.11.45	86	1913	9541			18.05.48
7	1904	9489			11.09.41	80	1913	9542			18.05.48
8	1904	9490			18.12.40	81	1913	9543			20.01.48
9	1904	9491			18.12.40	82	1913	9544			25.06.48
10	1904	9492			12.10.43	83	1913	9545			15.07.48
11	1904	9493			10.01.41	77	1913	9546	C		09.10.50
12	1904	9494			06.12.40	78	1913	9547	C		30.10.50
13	1904	9495			24.11.40	79	1913	9548	C		13.11.50
14	1904	9496			27.02.41	87	1921	9549	C		13.11.50
15	1904	9497			30.08.41	88	1921	9550	C		30.10.50
16	1904	9498			10.01.41	89	1921	9551	C		27.11.50
17	1904	9499			16.07.46	90	1921	9552	C		23.10.50
18	1904	9500			28.07.45	91	1921	9553	C		14.02.51
19	1904	9501			02.12.40	92	1921	9554	C		05.03.51
20	1904	9502			12.11.40	93	1921	9555	C		05.03.51
21	1904	9503			18.11.40	94	1921	9556	C		15.01.51
22	1904	9504			12.11.40	95	1921	9557	C		16.04.51
23	1904	9505			01.05.36	96	1921	9558	C		23.10.50
24	1904	9506			18.11.40	97	1921	9559	C		08.01.51
25	1904	9507			12.11.40	98	1921	9560	C		20.11.50
26	1904	9508			10.01.41	99	1921	9561	C		27.03.51
27	1904	9509			10.04.46	100	1921	9562	C		20.02.51
28	1904	9510			18.07.45	101	1921	9563	C		08.01.51
29	1904	9511			26.08.40	102	1921	9564	C		14.03.51
30	1904	9512			24.11.40	103	1921	9565	C		07.11.50
31	1905	9513			12.10.43	104	1921	9566	C		04.12.50
32	1905	9514			26.08.40	105	1921	9567	C		04.12.50
33	1905	9515			07.03.44	106	1921	9568	C		27.11.50
35	1905	9516			24.02.41	107	1921	9569	C		15.01.51
36	1905	9517			04.01.41	108	1921	9570	C		20.11.50
51	1905	9518			28.07.45	109	1921	9571	C		14.03.51
52	1905	9519			26.08.40	110	1921	9572	C		26.02.51
53	1905	9520			08.05.46	111	1921	9573	C		07.11.50
54	1905	9521			04.01.41	112	1921	9574	C		20.02.51
55	1905	9522			30.08.41	113	1921	9575	C		30.10.50
56	1905	9523			24.02.41	114	1921	9576	C		11.12.50
57	1906	9524			17.07.43	115	1921	9577	C		11.12.50
58	1906	9525			05.07.41	116	1921	9578	C		11.11.50
59	1906	9526			10.01.41	117	1921	9579	C		26.02.51
61	1906	9527			03.03.42	118	1921	9580	C		14.02.51
63	1906	9528			12.11.40	119	1921	9581	C		14.03.51

TRAILERS CONVERTED FROM MOTOR COACHES 1929–31:

Met. No.	Built	MR Reno.	LT No.	Disposal	Met No.	Built	MR Reno.	LT No.	Disposal
2	1904	191	9582	26.08.40	4	1904	200	9591	30.10.43
13	1904	192	9583	06.03.44	49	1905	201	9592	06.03.44
21	1904	193	9584	26.08.40	45	1905	202	9593	26.08.40
26	1904	194	9585	17.07.43	1	1904	203	9594	12.10.43
29	1904	195	9586	06.12.40	27	1904	204	9595	06.03.44
39	1905	196	9587	06.03.44	15	1904	205	9596	10.01.41
36	1905	197	9588	27.02.41	12	1904	206	9597	26.08.40
44	1905	198	9589	24.02.41	48	1905	207	9598	06.03.44
10	1904	199	9590	12.11.40	55	1905	208	9599	30.10.43

RENUMBERED FROM DRIVING TRAILERS:

Met. No.	Built	LT No.	Reno.	Date	Disposal	Met No.	Built	LT No.	Reno.	Date	Disposal
38	1906	6591	9479	26.01.35	24.11.40	46	1906	6595	9481	16.02.35	26.08.40
44	1906	6594	9480	21.01.35	10.03.43	48	1906	6597	9482	23.02.35	18.07.45

C Circle Line stock.
§ Cars loaned to GN&CR.
† Car converted for use on Mersey Railway.
# Replacement for original motor car No.18 of 1904.
‡ Cars fitted with experimental Metadyne equipment.
* To composite trailers in 1912, numbered respectively 1, 2, 3, 4, 7, 8, 9 and 10.

HAMMERSMITH & CITY LINE STOCK
DRIVING MOTOR COACHES – 48

MOTOR COACHES FROM 'MAIN LINE' STOCK:

Met. No.	Built	LT No.	Disposal	Met. No.	Built	LT No.	Disposal
71	1906	2200	† 21.02.46	81	1906	2204	24.10.38
73	1906	2201	17.02.38	76	1906	2205	22.09.38
80	1906	2202	27.01.43	82	1906	2206	10.06.38
74	1906	2203	30.10.43	79	1906	2207	† 03.09.45

HAMMERSMITH & CITY MOTOR COACHES:

H&C No.	Met. Rly Reno.	LT No.	Disposal	H&C No.	Met. Rly Reno.	LT No.	Disposal	H&C No.	Met. Rly Reno.	LT No.	Disposal
1	126	2208	17.12.40	15	140	2222	03.06.38	29	154	2236	10.04.42
2	127	2209	12.02.41	16	141	2223	26.05.38	30	155	2237	10.06.38
3	128	2210	03.06.38	17	142	2224	10.06.38	31	156	2238	12.02.41
4	129	2211	24.10.38	18	143	2225	27.01.43	32	157	2239	† 22.11.45
5	130	2212	22.09.38	19	144	2226	30.09.38	33	158	2240	27.01.43
6	131	2213	01.09.42	20	145	2227	† 21.02.46	34	159	2241	17.06.38
7	132	2214	27.02.41	21	146	2228	† 03.09.45	35	160	2242	01.09.42
8	133	2215	28.08.39	22	147	2229	07.05.38	36	161	2243	09.02.37
9	134	2216	28.08.39	23	148	2230	† 24.09.45	37	162	2244	21.07.38
10	135	2217	12.02.41	24	149	2231	12.02.41	38	163	2245	30.09.38
11	136	2218	20.12.40	25	150	2232	07.05.38	39	164	2246	25.11.42
12	137	2219	17.12.40	26	151	2233	† 24.09.45	40	165	2247	17.12.40
13	138	2220	17.12.40	27	152	2234	30.10.43				
14	139	2221	27.01.43	28	153	2235	19.11.42				

DRIVING TRAILERS – 49

DRIVING TRAILERS FROM 'MAIN LINE' STOCK:

Met. No.	Built	LT No.	Disposal	Met. No.	Built	LT No.	Disposal
28	1905	6201	03.03.42	39	1906	6221	21.07.38
76	1906	6203	†24.09.45	43	1906	6222	12.10.43
73	1906	6211	*†22.11.45	45	1906	6223	28.11.40
72	1906	6212	* 17.12.40	50	1906	6224	24.10.38
41	1906	6220	17.02.38				

HAMMERSMITH & CITY DRIVING TRAILERS:

No.	Met. Built	LT No.	Disposal	No.	Met. Built	LT No.	Disposal	No.	Met. Built	LT No.	Disposal
1	120	6225	30.09.38	15	134	6239	26.05.38	29	148	6253	06.12.40
2	121	6226	03.06.38	16	135	6240	02.12.40	30	149	6254	† 03.09.45
3	122	6227	22.09.38	17	136	6241	† 21.02.46	31	150	6255	† 21.02.46
4	123	6228	17.06.38	18	137	6242	26.05.38	32	151	6256	02.12.40
5	124	6229	07.05.38	19	138	6243	02.12.40	33	152	6257	27.07.38
6	125	6230	18.12.40	20	139	6244	17.12.40	34	153	6258	30.09.38
7	126	6231	20.12.40	21	140	6245	24.10.38	35	154	6259	† 03.09.45
8	127	6232	24.03.41	22	141	6246	07.05.38	36	155	6260	21.07.38
9	128	6233	29.01.42	23	142	6247	03.06.38	37	156	6261	22.09.38
10	129	6234	18.11.40	24	143	6248	28.11.40	38	157	6262	20.12.40
11	130	6235	05.07.41	25	144	6249	06.12.40	39	158	6263	10.06.38
12	131	6236	10.06.38	26	145	6250	18.11.40	40	159	6264	07.01.41
13	132	6237	20.12.40	27	146	6251	18.12.40				
14	133	6238	† 24.09.45	28	147	6252	27.07.38				

TRAILERS – 47

TRAILERS FROM 'MAIN LINE' STOCK:

Met. No.	Built	LT No.	Disposal	Met. No.	Built	LT No.	Disposal
62	1906	9200	17.06.38	34	1906	9210	21.03.38
67	1906	9201	17.02.38	60	1906	9211	18.12.40
68	1906	9202	29.06.36	62	1906	9212	26.08.40
69	1906	9203	17.12.40				

HAMMERSMITH & CITY TRAILERS:

H&C No.	Met. Rly Reno.	LT No.	Disposal	H&C No.	Met. Rly Reno.	LT No.	Disposal	H&C No.	Met. Rly Reno.	LT No.	Disposal
40	50	9220	† 03.09.45	14	24	9234	17.06.38	28	38	9248	27.07.38
1	11	9221	26.04.38	15	25	9235	26.05.38	29	39	9249	24.10.38
2	12	9222	† 22.11.45	16	26	9236	03.06.38	30	40	9250	20.12.40
3	13	9223	30.09.38	17	27	9237	10.06.38	31	41	9251	21.07.38
4	14	9224	† 21.02.46	18	28	9238	10.01.41	32	42	9252	02.12.40
5	15	9225	07.05.38	19	29	9239	06.12.40	33	43	9253	27.07.38
6	16	9226	18.12.40	20	30	9240	07.05.38	34	44	9254	22.09.38
7	17	9227	26.04.38	21	31	9241	† 21.02.46	35	45	9255	† 03.09.45
8	18	9228	† 24.09.45	22	32	9242	26.04.38	36	46	9256	24.10.38
9	19	9229	26.04.38	23	33	9243	03.06.38	37	47	9257	23.11.44
10	20	9230	22.09.38	24	34	9244	17.06.38	38	48	9258	07.01.41
11	21	9231	† 22.11.45	25	35	9245	26.04.38	39	49	9259	† 24.09.45
12	22	9232	10.06.38	26	36	9246	26.04.38				
13	23	9233	17.06.38	27	37	9247	30.09.38				

† Cars converted for use on Mersey Railway.
* To composite trailers in 1912 numbered respectively 6 and 5.

GREAT NORTHERN & CITY LINE STOCK
DRIVING MOTOR COACHES – 32

GN&C No.	Met. Rly Reno.	LT No.	Disposal	GN&C No.	Met. Rly Reno.	LT No.	Disposal	GN&C No.	Met. Rly Reno.	LT No.	Disposal
13†	167	2900	07.06.39	29	187	2911	16.06.39	21	179	2922	24.06.39
84*	166	2901	31.05.39	16	174	2912	16.06.39	22	180	2924	24.06.39
10	169	2902	05.06.35	30	188	2913	07.06.39	23	181	2926	16.06.39
9	168	2903	05.06.35	17	175	2914	24.06.39	26	184	2928	31.05.39
11	170	2904	01.07.39	36	194	2915	24.06.39	27	185	2930	24.06.39
24	182	2905	31.05.39	18	176	2916	31.05.39	31	189	2932	16.06.39
12	171	2906	24.05.39	37	195	2917	07.06.39	32	190	2934	07.06.39
25	183	2907	24.05.39	19	177	2918	07.06.39	33	191	2936	01.07.39
14	172	2908	31.05.39	38	196	2919	01.07.39	34	192	2938	30.11.37
28	186	2909	16.06.39	20	178	2920	24.05.39	35	193	2940	30.11.37
15	173	2910	01.07.39	39	197	2921	24.05.39				

* Originally trailer car – converted to motor coach No.7 in 1907.
† Renumbered 8 after accident.

DRIVING TRAILERS – 12

GN&C No.	Met. Rly Reno.	LT No.	Disposal	GN&C No.	Met. Rly Reno.	LT No.	Disposal	GN&C No.	Met. Rly Reno.	LT No.	Disposal
47	167	6900	30.11.37	42	162	6905	24.05.39	46	166	6913	24.06.39
40	160	6901	16.06.39	43	163	6907	31.05.39	48	168	6915	31.05.39
56	172	6902	24.05.39	44	164	6909	24.06.39	67	177	6917	01.07.39
41	161	6903	07.06.39	45	165	6911	29.04.36	71	178	6919	07.06.39

TRAILERS – 32

FIRST CLASS TRAILERS:

GN&C No.	Met. Rly Reno.	LT No.	Disposal	GN&C No.	Met. Rly Reno.	LT No.	Disposal	GN&C No.	Met. Rly Reno.	LT No.	Disposal
52	93	9900	31.05.39	58	98	9905	24.05.39	68	103	9910	01.07.39
53	94	9901	04.04.36	59	99	9906	16.06.39	69	104	9911	24.05.39
54	95	9902	07.06.39	63	100	9907	01.07.39	70	105	9912	29.04.36
55	96	9903	25.03.36	64	101	9908	29.04.36				
57	97	9904	04.04.36	65	102	9909	17.04.36				

THIRD CLASS TRAILERS:

GN&C No.	Met. Rly Reno.	LT No.	Disposal	GN&C No.	Met. Rly Reno.	LT No.	Disposal	GN&C No.	Met. Rly Reno.	LT No.	Disposal
49	169	9950	24.06.39	72	179	9957	24.05.39	79	186	9964	25.03.36
50	170	9951	26.09.38	73	180	9958	17.04.36	80	187	9965	11.03.37
51	171	9952	26.09.38	74	181	9959	25.03.36	81	188	9966	04.04.36
60	173	9953	16.06.39	75	182	9960	04.04.36	82	189	9967	26.04.39
61	174	9954	01.07.39	76	183	9961	26.09.38	83	190	9968	29.04.36
62	175	9955	17.04.36	77	184	9962	11.03.37				
66	176	9956	17.04.36	78	185	9963	25.03.36				

CHAPTER TWO

DISTRICT RAILWAY B, C, D AND E STOCKS

1905 B STOCK

The Metropolitan District Railway had experimented with electric traction between Earl's Court and High Street Kensington in 1899–1900, as had the Metropolitan Railway at Wembley Park in 1899. The District went a stage further by using the 3rd/4th rail system on the Ealing – South Harrow line which opened in 1903 and for which two seven-car trains were built by Brush (the A stock) in that year. The success of this resulted in the District deciding to eliminate steam traction and electrify its lines on that system. The lines involved comprised: Ealing/Hounslow – Whitechapel, plus the branches to High Street Kensington and South Acton.

For these services, a total of 420 new cars were required to form 60x7-car trains, of which 12 trains would comprise four motor cars and 48 trains three motor cars. This resulted in 192 motor cars and 228 trailers being ordered, following the typical American design with clerestory roofs, tapering downwards at the car ends. There were three types of motor cars provided out of the total of 192. Twenty were single-ended with a luggage compartment, 100 were single ended without a luggage compartment and 72 motor cars had a cab at each end (known as 'middle' motors). The 'middle' motor cars were located thus in a normal length train, facilitating easy coupling and uncoupling. They were also ideal for single car working on lightly used services and for that purpose, eight were designated to operate as such.

Unlike the Metropolitan, whose saloon type coaches were numbered upwards from '1' for each variant, the District had a separate series of numbers for each type. The numbering system itself was quite simple, but more difficult to comprehend was the way it was applied because of the number of different car builders

During the 1920s, many of the B stock motor cars of 1905 were converted to trailers and reconditioned, replacing many of the original wooden-bodied B stock trailers, whose condition was giving cause for concern. What remained of the original cars were retained on District shuttle services at the west end of the line. Seen at South Harrow (old station), a B stock train (right) on a shuttle service to Uxbridge stands next to a Piccadilly Line train, soon after the extension of the latter services from Hammersmith. District trains continued to operate to Uxbridge until October 1933. *Charles F. Klapper/LURS*

involved. In the UK, 70 cars were built by Brush in Loughborough and 70 by Metropolitan Amalgamated, while the remaining 280 were constructed in France. This was under the auspices of Les Ateliers de Construction du Nord de la France, whose main works were at Blanc Misseron, but some cars were built at other workshops at Ivry, Luneville, Pantin and Saint-Denis. The cars were 49ft 6½in long and were 8ft 10½in wide at maximum. Each car had a pair of double doors in the centre along with single doors at each end (trailers) or one end (motors). With all the various different builders involved with the construction of the B stock, they were remarkably identical. An innovation at the time was that the passenger doors were air-operated under control of a 'gateman'. This was far from successful and the system was removed in 1908 with doors then being hand-operated. Air doors were not to feature on 'surface' stock again until 1935, although it was tried on the 1920 Cammell Laird 'tube' stock and subsequently incorporated on all new tube stock built from 1922.

The following is a list of the cars, how they were numbered and who built them. The numbers allocated began after those of the A stock of 1903.

End Motors:

Brush	5, 10, 15 and in sequence up to 100*
Met Amalgamated	6–9, 11–14, 16–19, 21–24, 26–29
Lunneville	31–34, 36–39, 41–44, 46–49, 51–54
Blanc Misseron	56–59, 61–64, 66–69, 71–74, 76–79, 81–84, 86–89, 91–94
	96–99, 101–104, 106–109, 111–114, 116–119, 121–124,
	126–129

* All 20 cars originally provided with luggage compartments.

Middle Motors:

Brush	203–214
Met Amalgamated	215–220, 222–226, 264
Lunneville	221, 227–263, 265–274

Trailers:

Brush	309–346
Met Amalgamated	347–384
Pantin	385–404, 470–480, 526–536
Ivry Port	405–425, 481–501
Saint-Denis	426–469, 502–525

All car bodies were built of wood, but the motor cars had steel under-frames onto which the wooden bodies were constructed. The livery was mostly maroon, with the window frames and doors varnished to exploit the natural wood colour. Inside the cars, first class seating was luxurious, but third class seats had rattan upholstery. The longitudinal seats originally did not have armrests, but these were later fitted to ensure fair play in seating provision! The car ends were fitted with pantograph-type protection barriers to prevent passengers from falling between cars – some tube stock cars were fitted with chains. These later fell into disuse and most were removed – only now, over 90 years later has this safety feature been reintroduced – the wheel thus turns full circle!

A total of 32 out of the 228 trailers were in fact control trailers, 11 being single-ended, the remaining 21 being double-ended, the latter often working on the District Railway shuttles at the west end of the line.

Very soon, it was found necessary to fit (sliding) doors between the passenger saloon and the entrance vestibules. This served two purposes. Firstly it reduced draughts in the passenger saloon and secondly it discouraged passengers from travelling on the end platforms. This work began from the end of 1906.

Repainting from the summer of 1907 saw a number of cars emerge in green livery but this was soon deemed unsatisfactory and repainting reverted to the standard vermilion by the autumn of the same year. From 1910 work began on converting the luggage compartments for passenger use, increasing the seating capacity by eight in each car. The sliding doors of the luggage compartment were replaced by ordinary saloon windows. Also undertaken at the same time was the fitting of continuous footboards, rather than just at doorway positions.

From 1908, holders for train set numbers, destination and non-stop plates were fitted and work began on providing first class accommodation. The latter work continued through to 1914 and ultimately comprised 130 cars. Non-stopping services began in 1907 and were expanded in 1911, and all cars had been fitted with proper 'Not stopping at' boards between 1912–13 to reduce passenger confusion as to which train passed which station(s).

The B stock had five headlights, which were used to display a code according to the destination of the train. Two were provided at each side under the cab windows at the corners and a fifth above the centre cab door. This single headlight was later relocated to the top of the offside cab window, the size of which was reduced at the top in consequence.

The subsequent history of the B stock is rather complex and only a summary will be attempted. Suffice to say that in the early days, many motor cars underwent conversions, as more stock arrived.

From the total of 192 motor coaches, three had been scrapped (one each in 1911, 1916 and 1922) as the result of collisions, leaving 189 in stock. The deteriorating condition of the wooden-bodied trailers saw a number of these scrapped from 1922. Between 1922 and 1925, the original A stock was also scrapped. When the G stock motor cars arrived in 1924–25, a total of 42 B stock motor cars were converted to trailers, leaving 147. Another 110 were converted to trailers in 1928–30 in a re-modernisation plan for the District Railway stock, with further wooden-bodied trailers being scrapped. After this programme, there remained just 37 motor cars of B stock for service and 248 trailers. Of the latter, 152 were conversions from former motor cars and 96 were reconditioned original trailers. The delivery of new stock, however, saw numbers continue to reduce in the 1930s. In June 1930, four withdrawn trailer cars (412, 415, 416 and 424) were adapted to serve as Stores Cars and survived as such until scrapped in 1938.

The District Railway had always given its electric stock letters as a means of identification. The reconditioned B stock trailers took the next letter available and became the H stock. The original unmodified B stock was also known as 'local' stock, on which services they worked, being incompatible with modernised cars. The new and reconditioned (H stock) cars were also known as 'steel' stock. It is interesting to note that when the H stock was withdrawn, this letter was afterwards re-used collectively to identify later-built cars that still had hand worked doors, indicating **H**andworked door stock.

In 1932, motor car 37 was converted for single-car operation on the South Acton–Acton Town shuttle service. This involved providing air-operated doors in both cabs under control of the motorman – guards were not provided on this single-car service. This car continued in service until May 1941, when it was replaced by converted G stock motor cars. The few remaining complete trains of B stock at that time were then confined to 'local' services at the west end of the District and much of what remained had been withdrawn by the outbreak of the Second World War, although some of it survived until after hostilities had ceased. Motor car No.31 (ex-84) was the last to survive in as near-original form. In 1935, motor car No.8 (ex-No.55) and control trailer 1712 (ex-No.362) were converted into a two-car weed-killing train. The driving trailer was replaced in 1937 by motor car No.10, the control trailer being scrapped the following year. The two weed-killing motor cars survived until scrapped in February 1950.

Summary of disposal of B stock:

	Cars scrapped	Total scrapped	In stock		Cars scrapped	Total scrapped	In stock
As delivered	–	–	420				
At LPTB formation	133	133	287				
By end year				By end year			
1933	11	144	276	1940	72	385	35
1934	1	145	275	1941	1	386	34
1935	10	155	265	1944	1	387	33
1936	20	175	245	1945	23	410	10
1937	6	181	239	1946	5	415	5
1938	46	227	193	1948	3	418	2
1939	86	313	107	1950	2	420	–

UNREFURBISHED DRIVING MOTOR COACHES – 37

Previous Final DR No.	No.		Builder	Motor Car Type	Disposal	Previous Final DR No.	No.		Builder	Motor Car Type	Disposal
40	1	*	Brush	End	29.02.40		20	*	Brush	End	18.01.40
45	2	*	Brush	End	29.06.35		21		MAR	End	27.03.40
50	3	*	Brush	End	01.07.38	68	22		Blanc Misseron	End	06.02.40
51	4		Lunneville	End	29.06.35	70	23	*	Brush	End	29.02.40
	5	*	Brush	End	02.02.39	75	24	*	Brush	End	29.02.40
	6		MAR	End	29.06.35		25	*	Brush	End	06.02.40
	7		MAR	End	04.03.38	80	26	*	Brush	End	29.06.35
55	8	‡*Brush		End	27.02.50		27		MAR	End	06.10.38
	9		MAR	End	06.02.40		28		MAR	End	10.09.45
	10	‡	Brush	End	27.02.50	85	29	*	Brush	End	04.03.38
	11		MAR	End	13.04.39		30	*	Brush	End	20.10.38
60	12	*	Brush	End	29.06.35	84	31		Blanc Misseron	End	05.02.48
63	13		Blanc Misseron	End	18.01.40	90	32	*	Brush	End	29.06.35
65	14	*	Brush	End	26.04.38	95	33	*	Brush	End	26.04.38
	15	*	Brush	End	18.01.40	100	34	*	Brush	End	06.10.38
	16		MAR	End	29.06.35		35	*	Brush	End	09.02.46
	17		MAR	End	29.06.35	237	36	†	Lunneville	Middle	04.03.38
66	18		Blanc Misseron	End	27.03.40	233	37	†	Lunneville	Middle	10.02.48
67	19		Blanc Misseron	End	29.06.35						

* Motor cars originally provided with luggage compartments.
† 233 became 36 in 1929 and 37 in 1930. In 1930 237 became 36.
‡ Converted to Weed Killing cars in 1935 (No.8) and 1937 (No.10).

UNREFURBISHED TRAILER CARS – 77

Orig. No.	Reno. 1926–30	Builder	Disposal	Orig. No.	Reno. 1926–30	Builder	Disposal
311	1000	Brush	09.04.40	343	1020	Brush	16.02.39
312	1001	Brush	28.01.37	347	1021	MAR	26.11.36
313	1002	Brush	26.06.40	348	1022	MAR	16.02.39
316	1003	Brush	26.11.36	351	1024	MAR	01.05.40
317	1004	Brush	28.10.36	352	1025	MAR	16.02.39
318	1005	Brush	11.11.39	355	1026	MAR	28.01.37
319	1006	Brush	15.12.38	356	1027	MAR	28.01.37
321	1007	Brush	16.01.39	357	1028	MAR	01.07.38
322	1008	Brush	29.02.40	363	1029	MAR	28.10.36
324	1010	Brush	15.12.38	365	1030	MAR	23.12.36
331	1012	Brush	26.11.36	368	1031	MAR	27.02.39
332	1013	Brush	28.10.36	372	1032	MAR	28.01.37
334	1014	Brush	23.12.36	373	1033	MAR	26.11.36
335	1015	Brush	26.04.38	389	1035	Pantin	09.04.40
336	1016	Brush	16.02.39	390	1036	Pantin	28.01.37
339	1018	Brush	27.02.39	391	1037	Pantin	26.11.36
341	1019	Brush	28.10.36	395	1038	Pantin	17.07.39

397	**1039**	Pantin	19.06.40		474	**1065**	Pantin	02.02.39
398	**1040**	Pantin	31.10.39		475	**1066**	Pantin	25.07.39
400	**1041**	Pantin	08.05.40		476	**1067**	Pantin	08.05.40
403	**1042**	Pantin	28.01.37		477	**1068**	Pantin	11.11.39
404	**1043**	Pantin	27.02.39		426	**1069**	Saint-Denis	01.05.40
405	**1044**	Ivry Port	04.03.38		481	**1072**	Ivry Port	27.03.40
406	**1045**	Ivry Port	02.02.39		487	**1073**	Ivry Port	26.06.40
407	**1046**	Ivry Port	23.01.39		490	**1074**	Ivry Port	12.06.39
410	**1047**	Ivry Port	02.02.39		495	**1075**	Ivry Port	06.10.38
436	**1049**	Saint-Denis	27.02.39		496	**1076**	Ivry Port	02.02.39
440	**1050**	Saint-Denis	28.10.36		502	**1077**	Saint-Denis	23.12.36
443	**1051**	Saint-Denis	23.12.36		507	**1079**	Saint-Denis	16.10.39
445	**1052**	Saint-Denis	11.11.39		429	**1082**	Saint-Denis	31.10.39
448	**1053**	Saint-Denis	23.12.36		430	**1083**	Saint-Denis	17.11.39
449	**1054**	Saint-Denis	01.05.40		432	**1085**	Saint-Denis	28.08.39
454	**1056**	Saint-Denis	27.03.40		433	**1086**	Saint-Denis	26.11.36
455	**1057**	Saint-Denis	23.12.36		414	**1087**	Ivry Port	01.05.40
457	**1058**	Saint-Denis	13.04.39		411	**1088***	Ivry Port	15.12.38
458	**1059**	Saint-Denis	28.10.36		528	**1091**	Pantin	17.11.39
460	**1060**	Saint-Denis	28.10.36		530	**1093**	Pantin	27.02.39
469	**1061**	Saint-Denis	26.11.36		531	**1094**	Pantin	13.04.39
472	**1063**	Pantin	15.12.38					

UNREFURBISHED CONTROL TRAILERS – 18

Orig. No.	Reno. 1926–30	Builder	Type	Disposal	Orig. No.	Reno. 1926–30	Builder	Type	Disposal
315	**1700**	Brush	DE	24.04.45	354	**1709**	MAR	DE	26.04.38
327	**1701**	Brush	DE	18.01.40	358	**1710**	MAR	SE	12.06.39
333	**1702**	Brush	SE	18.01.40	360	**1711**	MAR	DE	17.11.39
340	**1703**	Brush	DE	04.08.38	362	**1712***	MAR	SE	Mar-38
342	**1704**	Brush	SE	29.02.40	364	**1713**	MAR	SE	27.02.40
345	**1705**	Brush	SE	04.03.38	370	**1714**	MAR	SE	06.02.40
326	**1706†**	Brush	SE	29.06.35	380	**1715**	MAR	DE	26.04.38
349	**1707**	MAR	DE	29.02.40	382	**1716**	MAR	DE	18.01.40
353	**1708**	MAR	DE	06.02.40	387	**1717**	Pantin	DE	06.02.40

* Converted to Weed Killing car in 1935.
† Converted from trailer 1011 in 1932.
DE – Double-ended.   SE – Single-ended.

TRAILERS CONVERTED FROM MOTOR CARS – 140

Orig. No.	Reno. 1923–25	Reno. 1926–30	Reno. 1930–32	LT No.	Builder	Ex-Motor Car Type	Disposal
238	1416	816		**8200**	Lunneville	Middle	19.06.45
220	1417	817		**8201**	MAR	Middle	16.07.40
232	1418	818		**8202**	Lunneville	Middle	16.01.39
249	1420	820		**8203**	Lunneville	Middle	26.06.40
236	1423	823		**8204**	Lunneville	Middle	01.06.45
240	1424	824		**8205**	Lunneville	Middle	17.11.39
251	1425	825		**8206**	Lunneville	Middle	24.04.40
243	1426	826		**8207**	Lunneville	Middle	25.05.45
230	1427	827		**8208**	Lunneville	Middle	03.07.40
254	1428	828		**8209**	Lunneville	Middle	16.10.39
241	1429	829		**8210**	Lunneville	Middle	25.02.41
234	1430	830		**8211**	Lunneville	Middle	06.07.45
252	1431	831		**8212**	Lunneville	Middle	16.10.39
213		881		**8213**	Brush	Middle	19.06.40
203		882		**8214**	Brush	Middle	24.04.40
204		883		**8215**	Brush	Middle	23.01.39

206		885		8216	Brush	Middle	16.07.40
207		886		8217	Brush	Middle	01.07.38
244		903		8218	Lunneville	Middle	16.01.39
245		904		8219	Lunneville	Middle	17.08.38
247		906		8220	Lunneville	Middle	24.04.40
253		908		8221	Lunneville	Middle	19.06.40
256		909		8222	Lunneville	Middle	03.07.40
257		910		8223	Lunneville	Middle	26.06.40
258		911		8224	Lunneville	Middle	19.06.40
259		912		8225	Lunneville	Middle	13.04.39
263	1600	915		8226	Lunneville	Middle	24.04.40
269	1601	916		8227	Lunneville	Middle	24.04.40
270	1603	918		8228	Lunneville	Middle	16.07.40
273	1604	919		8229	Lunneville	Middle	24.04.45
221	1605	920		8230	Lunneville	Middle	31.10.39
272	1606	921		8231	Lunneville	Middle	27.01.48
268	1607	922		8232	Lunneville	Middle	03.07.40
265	1608	923		8233	Lunneville	Middle	06.06.45
274	1609	924		8234	Lunneville	Middle	01.07.38
217		925		8235	MAR	Middle	23.01.39
264		926		8236	MAR	Middle	10.09.45
222		927		8237	MAR	Middle	09.04.40
224		895	928	8238	MAR	Middle	19.06.40
225		929		8239	MAR	Middle	03.07.40
226		930		8240	MAR	Middle	09.04.40
227		931		8241	Lunneville	Middle	16.01.39
228		932		8242	Lunneville	Middle	24.04.40
223	1404	933		8243	MAR	Middle	16.10.39
248	1405	934		8244	Lunneville	Middle	01.06.45
266		936		8245	Lunneville	Middle	09.04.40
267		937		8246	Lunneville	Middle	05.05.40
216	1408	938		8247	MAR	Middle	19.06.39
255	1410	939		8248	Lunneville	Middle	25.05.45
231	1412	940		8249	Lunneville	Middle	19.06.45
205		884	941	8250	Brush	Middle	06.07.45
219		942		8251	MAR	Middle	12.06.39
37		943		8252	Lunneville	End	05.05.45
38		944		8253	Lunneville	End	31.10.39
39		945		8254	Lunneville	End	02.02.39
208		887	946	8255	Brush	Middle	11.11.39
46		947		8256	Lunneville	End	16.10.34
209		888	948	8257	Brush	Middle	11.11.39
210		889	949	8258	Brush	Middle	12.06.39
119	1400	800		8700	Blanc Misseron	End	19.06.39
121	1401	801		8701	Blanc Misseron	End	24.04.45
124	1402	802		8702	Blanc Misseron	End	27.05.39
127	1403	803		8703	Blanc Misseron	End	17.08.38
24		804		8704	MAR	End	31.10.39
26		805		8705	MAR	End	20.10.38
129		806		8706	Blanc Misseron	End	17.08.38
29		807		8707	MAR	End	12.07.39
31		808		8708	Lunneville	End	27.06.39
43		809		8709	Lunneville	End	16.06.45
32		810		8710	Lunneville	End	20.10.38
41		811		8711	Lunneville	End	16.02.39
33		812		8712	Lunneville	End	17.08.38
34		813		8713	Lunneville	End	15.12.38
42	1414	814		8714	Lunneville	End	12.06.39
36		815		8715	Lunneville	End	01.05.40
53		832		8716	Lunneville	End	06.09.39
54		833		8717	Lunneville	End	23.01.39
56		834		8718	Blanc Misseron	End	06.10.38

57	835			8719	Blanc Misseron	End	03.07.40
58	836			8720	Blanc Misseron	End	07.12.39
13	894	837		8721	MAR	End	09.02.46
61	838			8722	Blanc Misseron	End	15.12.38
62	839			8723	Blanc Misseron	End	08.05.40
64	840			8724	Blanc Misseron	End	17.08.38
69	841			8725	Blanc Misseron	End	15.12.45
71	842			8726	Blanc Misseron	End	26.06.40
72	843			8727	Blanc Misseron	End	20.10.38
73	844			8728	Blanc Misseron	End	05.05.45
74	845			8729	Blanc Misseron	End	16.07.44
76	846			8730	Blanc Misseron	End	02.11.45
77	847			8731	Blanc Misseron	End	19.06.39
78	848			8732	Blanc Misseron	End	11.11.39
79	849			8733	Blanc Misseron	End	28.08.39
81	850			8734	Blanc Misseron	End	27.06.39
82	851			8735	Blanc Misseron	End	27.06.39
83	852			8736	Blanc Misseron	End	08.05.40
88	853			8737	Blanc Misseron	End	16.01.39
86	854			8738	Blanc Misseron	End	05.05.46
87	855			8739	Blanc Misseron	End	26.06.40
89	856			8740	Blanc Misseron	End	20.10.38
92	857			8741	Blanc Misseron	End	12.06.39
93	858			8742	Blanc Misseron	End	27.03.40
96	859			8743	Blanc Misseron	End	27.06.39
97	860			8744	Blanc Misseron	End	16.07.40
98	861			8745	Blanc Misseron	End	27.06.39
99	862			8746	Blanc Misseron	End	16.01.39
101	863			8747	Blanc Misseron	End	10.09.45
102	864			8748	Blanc Misseron	End	01.07.38
103	865			8749	Blanc Misseron	End	19.06.40
104	866			8750	Blanc Misseron	End	20.10.38
106	867			8751	Blanc Misseron	End	28.08.39
107	868			8752	Blanc Misseron	End	10.09.45
108	869			8753	Blanc Misseron	End	03.07.40
109	870			8754	Blanc Misseron	End	19.06.39
111	871			8755	Blanc Misseron	End	08.05.40
112	872			8756	Blanc Misseron	End	16.10.39
113	873			8757	Blanc Misseron	End	27.05.39
114	874			8758	Blanc Misseron	End	08.05.40
116	875			8759	Blanc Misseron	End	23.01.39
117	876			8760	Blanc Misseron	End	28.05.38
118	877			8761	Blanc Misseron	End	19.06.39
122	878			8762	Blanc Misseron	End	23.01.39
123	879			8763	Blanc Misseron	End	06.07.45
44	946	887		8764	Lunneville	End	27.06.39
47	947	888		8765	Lunneville	End	17.08.38
48	948	889		8766	Lunneville	End	10.09.45
126	890			8767	Blanc Misseron	End	01.07.38
128	891			8768	Blanc Misseron	End	12.06.39
8	892			8769	MAR	End	27.03.40
12	893			8770	MAR	End	16.07.40
14	895			8771	MAR	End	12.07.39
18	896			8772	MAR	End	27.05.39
19	897			8773	MAR	End	09.04.40
22	898			8774	MAR	End	12.07.39
23	899			8775	MAR	End	01.05.40
239	901			8776	Lunneville	Middle	27.05.39
49	950			8777	Lunneville	End	06.10.38
262	914			8778	Lunneville	Middle	09.02.46
260	913	917		8779	Lunneville	Middle	09.02.46
214	1407	935		8780	Brush	Middle	27.05.39

1910–1913 C, D and E STOCK

Soon after the B stock of 1905 had entered service, it was necessary to make a number of modifications to the trains, to adapt to the service conditions and demands of what was then a new electric railway. The success of electrification also prompted the District Railway to undertake engineering projects, to enable services to be improved. These included:

- Resignalling of the central area, enabling certain non-stop services to be introduced (1907).
- Acton Town station rebuilt with a flying junction west of the station (1910).
- Segregation of District and L&SWR trains between west of Hammersmith and west of Turnham Green (1911).
- Flyunder junction west of Earl's Court (1914).
- Some train lengths increased from seven to eight cars.

In addition to non-stopping services, train lengths were also increased and these varied with the various experiments undertaken. Train lengths up to 12-cars were tried in 1911 – originating from East Ham, they divided at Whitechapel, the front portion operating a non-stop service, the rear an all stations service. Extensions from East Ham to Barking (1908) and South Harrow to Uxbridge (1910) required additional trains.

A C stock motor car built by Hurst Nelson in 1910 leads a train into High Street Kensington. These trains were collectively known as H stock in their later days (H – handworked door), although this letter had been previously used to distinguish the rehabilitated B stock in the 1920s. The leading car is 4214, which was previously a 'D'-end car until turned and converted in 1939. *F.G. Reynolds*

The D stock, built in 1911 by Metropolitan Amalgamated was remarkably similar to the C stock. Motor car 4065 leads a southbound East London Line train at Surrey Docks.
F.G. Reynolds

All of these changes and improvements therefore required additional rolling stock. Three batches were subsequently ordered, the first being what was designated as C stock. This was ordered in April 1910 and was built by Hurst Nelson of Motherwell. The order comprised 32 motor cars and 20 trailers. All cars were of a standard dimension, being 49ft 0in long and 8ft 9½in wide. They were quite similar to the B stock but differed in that the new stock was of all-steel construction, with wooden trimming. Interior improvements were made – inward tilting quarter lights were provided along with better lighting. The only distinctive difference between the B and C stocks was that the latter had no curved section at the top of the main car windows. Also, the top headlight, above the front communicating door on B stock, was relocated at the top of the offside cab window, which was thus smaller in size – the B stock motors and control trailers were subsequently modified in the same way.

A second order for new cars was placed in April 1911 with Metropolitan Amalgamated and initially was for 15 motors and 15 trailers. This was designated D stock but the order was subsequently changed to be for 22 motors and eight trailers. Despite being designated separately, the D stock cars were visibly identical to the C stock, only the thickness of the car window glass and the type of flooring made them 'different'.

The final batch of cars was the E stock, comprising 26 motor cars and four trailers. These were ordered in December 1912 from Gloucester. They resembled their predecessors up to roof level, but above, the hitherto traditional clerestory roof gave way to an elliptical roof, on top of which there were 'torpedo' ventilators. This feature was subsequently removed to reduce interior draughts.

The C, D and E stocks were collectively known as the 'Hurst Nelson' stock, although it was only the C stock that was in fact built by that company. The last had been delivered to provide rolling stock for the L&NWR, for its newly electrified services between Willesden Junction and Earl's Court, which was a small remnant of the 'Outer Circle' service. The District cars operated on the L&NWR service until the company's new EMU stock was ready – from 1 May to 22 November 1914. For those few months, the District stock for this service was stabled and maintained at the Piccadilly Line depot at Lillie Bridge (which was originally District Railway premises until 1905). The C, D and E types were compatible with the B stock although the latter type were wearing badly, especially the all-wooden trailers, where deterioration of the bodywork gave cause for concern.

The new stock was numbered as follows:

C Stock	Motor cars	169–200	32
	Trailers	537–556	20
D Stock	Motor cars	147–168	22
	Trailers	557–564	8
E Stock	Motor cars	275–300	26
	Trailers	565–568	4
			112

A four-car train of H stock is seen west of East Putney heading for Wimbledon in 1938. The first car is C or D stock, followed by a B stock trailer, then an L or N class trailer, with a K stock motor car at the rear. *Real Photographs Co. Ltd*

All of the C, D and E stock trailers were converted into motor cars between 1928 and 1930. This was in connection with the delivery of further new stock and the conversion of more of the wooden-bodied B stock motor cars into trailers. When the LPTB was formed there were a total of 112 motor cars within this group – 52 C stock, 30 D stock and 30 E stock, of which 20, eight and four respectively were former trailer cars. Those 32 that were converted from trailers followed the design of the new motor cars of the time, in having enclosed destination plates beneath the offside cab window, beneath which were the similarly enclosed group of headlights.

The decision to use the C, D and E types on the East London Line instead of the Metropolitan's own cars, resulted in a number of further conversions. The C stock was chosen for the conversion work and during 1938–39 seven of the original motor cars were converted into trailers, with a further eight becoming control trailers. Two motor cars were also 'turned' from east-facing to west-facing to balance the number of cars required for the District. District stock in fact began working on the East London Line from May 1937 but it was not until 1940 that the line had an 'official' allocation of C stock cars. One C stock motor car – 4028 – was written off after being involved in a collision with a Circle Line train near Charing Cross on 17 May 1938, as a result of a signal wiring fault.

The arrival of the R stock in 1949–52 resulted in much of the C, D and E stocks being withdrawn and scrapped. On the East London Line it was replaced by F stock. In the same programme was the conversion of hand-worked door L, M and N stock that ran with the older cars (q.v. below) to air-door operation. This resulted in ten motor cars (3 C stock, 3 D stock and 4 E stock) being converted into trailers, and one D stock motor car into a control trailer, all in 1950–51. Three of these conversions were on cars that originally had started life as trailers! At the end of the programme, sufficient cars of C, D and E stock were retained for the Earl's Court – Olympia shuttle, and a pair of motors for 'pilot' duties. However, the use of these old trains on what was deemed a prestige exhibition service was deemed unsatisfactory and they were officially withdrawn from service in February 1958 (4037, 4053, 4118, 4138, 8787, 8789, 8791 and 8902) and March 1958 (4139, 4214, 8799 and 8901), being the last hand-worked sliding door rolling stock on the Underground.

The following lists show the C, D and E stocks as inherited by the LPTB in 1933, followed by later conversions and renumbering.

The C, D and E stock trailers rebuilt as motor cars in the 1928–30 period differed from the original motor cars in a number of respects, the most obvious being the enclosed headlights and destination plates under the offside cab window. On the E stock, the rainstrip extended across the cab, unlike the original motors, where it was just over the cab door. *F.G. Reynolds*

C STOCK DRIVING MOTOR CARS – 52

Orig. No.		1928–30 Reno.	1932 Reno.	1930s No.	Conv. & Reno.	Date	Conv. & Reno.	Date	Disposal
181		112		4000	**8786**	23.05.38			16.12.53
171		101		4001	**8787**	23.05.38			
183		114		4002	**6100**	09.01.39			20.01.54
172		103		4003	**8789**	07.06.38			
185		116		4004	**6102**	10.10.38			06.01.54
175		105		4005	**8791**	27.06.38			
187		118		4006	**6104**	05.12.38			24.06.52
176		107		4007	**8793**	15.06.38			16.12.53
189		120		4008	**8794**	10.05.38			24.04.41
178		109		4009	8795	27.06.38	**6107**	10.06.39	16.07.52
191		122		4010	**6106**	08.07.39			20.01.54
180		111		4011	**4214**	15.07.38			
193		124		4012	**6101**	05.09.38			28.07.53
182		113		4013	**4216**	25.07.38			09.04.51
195		126		4014	**6103**	10.10.38			29.12.53
184		115		**4015**					19.07.51
197		128		4016	**6105**	20.09.38			16.09.52
186		117		**4017**					06.01.54
198		130		**4018**					10.06.52
188		119		**4019**					09.04.51
537	*	132		**4020**					24.06.52
190		121		**4021**					04.07.52
539	*	134		**4022**					10.02.54
192		123		**4023**					20.01.54
541	*	136		**4024**					15.10.52
194		125		**4025**					09.04.51
543	*	138		**4026**					28.07.53
196		127		**4027**					06.01.54
545	*	140		**4028**					17.06.38
199		129		**4029**					29.12.56
547	*	142		**4030**					29.12.56
200		131		4031	**8901**	23.12.50			
549	*	144		**4032**					19.07.51
538	*	133		**4033**					16.12.53
551	*	146		**4034**					30.11.53
540	*	135		4035	**8903**	12.03.51			13.11.53
553	*	148		**4036**					18.06.52
542	*	137		**4037**					
555	*	150		**4038**					10.06.52
544	*	139		**4039**					04.07.52
546	*	141		**4041**					24.04.41
548	*	143		**4043**					10.11.50
550	*	145		4045	**8799**	06.01.50			
552	*	147		**4047**					16.07.52
554	*	149		**4049**					20.01.54
556	*	151		**4051**					29.12.53
169		100	231	**4053**					
170		102	233	**4055**					09.04.51
173		104	235	**4057**					15.10.52
174		106	237	**4059**					29.12.53
177		108	239	**4061**					19.08.52
179		110	241	**4063**					16.07.52

* Originally built as trailer cars. Converted to motor cars 1928–30.

D STOCK DRIVING MOTOR CARS – 30

Orig. No.	1928–30 Reno.		1930s No.	Conv. & Reno.	Date	Disposal
147	152		4064			24.04.41
148	153		4065			06.01.54
149	154		4066			03.09.52
150	155		4067			10.06.52
151	156		4068			16.12.53
152	157		4069			28.07.53
162	158		4070	**8797**	29.11.50	28.07.53
153	159		4071			28.07.53
163	160		4072			24.06.52
164	161		4073	**6109**	10.06.50	16.09.52
165	162		4074	**8796**	06.11.50	06.01.54
166	163		4075			10.06.52
167	164		4076	**8902**	20.01.51	
168	165		4077			04.07.52
154	167		4079			04.07.52
155	169		4081			03.09.52
156	171		4083			19.08.52
157	173		4085			15.10.52
158	175		4087			12.10.50
159	177		4089			18.06.52
160	179		4091			16.09.52
161	181		4093			20.09.50
557	*	183	4095			03.09.52
558	*	185	4097			24.04.41
559	*	187	4099			24.06.52
560	*	189	4101			03.09.52
561	*	191	4103			19.07.51
562	*	193	4105			10.02.54
563	*	195	4107			19.07.51
564	*	197	4109			19.07.51

* Originally built as trailer cars. Converted to motor cars 1928–30.

A four-car train of District H stock in post-war days on the Metropolitan's East London Line departs from Surrey Docks, with all four cars comprising C or D stock. The rear motor car is one that was converted from a trailer in 1928–30, hence the much neater arrangement of the destination plates and headlights. Because there are no air-worked doors, the guard is seen riding in the rear cab. In hot weather, these trains had their own air-conditioning – the train doors were left open! *F.G. Reynolds*

E STOCK DRIVING MOTOR CARS – 30

Orig. No.	1928–30 Reno.	1930s No.	Conv. & Reno.	Date	Disposal
275	200	4110			16.12.53
276	201	4111			16.07.52
277	202	4112			19.08.52
278	203	4113			04.07.52
279	204	4114			19.08.52
280	205	4115	8904	24.02.51	24.06.52
281	206	4116			18.06.52
282	207	4117			16.07.52
283	208	4118			
284	209	4119			16.09.52
285	210	4120			30.11.53
286	211	4121			18.06.52
287	212	4122			14.08.52
288	213	4123			18.06.52
289	214	4124			10.06.52
290	215	4125			30.11.53
291	216	4126			16.09.52
292	217	4127			15.10.52
293	218	4128			29.12.53
294	219	4129			05.09.52
295	220	4130			20.01.54
296	221	4131			09.04.51
297	222	4132	8798	18.11.50	14.08.52
298	223	4133			03.09.52
299	224	4134			10.02.54
300	225	4135	8900	14.12.50	29.12.53
565	* 226	4136	8795	21.10.50	10.02.54
566	* 227	4137			19.08.52
567	* 228	4138			
568	* 229	4139			

* Originally built as trailer cars. Converted to motor cars 1928–30.

The 1914 E stock built by Gloucester broke tradition and was built with elliptical roofs. The diversity of District stock is illustrated in this mixed formation six-car train arriving at East Ham on 29 June 1950. When originally built the E class cars had 'torpedo' ventilators on the roof, but were soon removed because they caused draughts. *Author's collection*

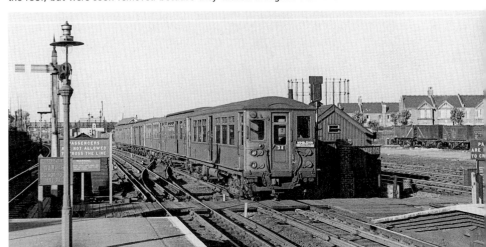

CHAPTER THREE

DISTRICT RAILWAY F STOCK

It was the desire to improve capacity and increase service performance, especially because of the growing traffic in west London, that led to the purchase of 100 cars of F stock, coupled with the fact that the wooden-bodied B stock trailers of 1905 were in a serious condition of deterioration. The order was placed in 1919 by the District Railway with the Metropolitan Carriage, Wagon & Finance Co. and comprised 40 double-ended driving motor cars, 12 single-ended composite control trailers and 48 trailers (of which 12 were composite). Each type of car had seats for 40, 44 and 48 passengers respectively. The F stock introduced a number of different features to 'surface' rolling stock. Apart from being slightly longer than its predecessors, the flush-panelled sides sloped slightly inwards above waist level, to fit within the loading gauge, and the width below the waist was 9ft 7in. The absence of footboards allowed the cars to be built this wide. Even so, some remedial work on station platforms had to be undertaken before the trains could enter service – hitherto, District Railway stock had straight sides. Each car had three double doors per side, the centre pair having non-stop boards on each side. Coupled with a large proportion of longitudinal seating in each car – only the two bays at the car ends had transverse seating – the F stock had a huge appetite for carrying large numbers of passengers. Driving cab windows were oval in shape – this must have been the fashion at the time as the 1920 Cammell Laird tube cars of similar vintage also had this feature, as did stock built just after for the Berlin U-Bahn. On the District F stock, however, the inner car ends also had oval windows thus giving a feeling of spaciousness as well as being light and airy. Communicating doors were changed to be hinged and inward opening instead of side sliding. The cars were originally numbered:

600–639	Driving motor cars, double-ended, double-equipped.
900–911	Control trailers.
1000–1011	Trailers, 1st/3rd class.
1100–1135	Trailers, 3rd class.

The F stock on the District originally operated in 5+3-car sets, to facilitate uncoupling at Acton Town, but were later formed into four-car sets. One such formation is seen arriving at East Ham, heading for Acton Town.
Author's collection

Official records show that the F stock first entered passenger service on 23 December 1920, but this was trailer cars only, the first four of which were delivered on 19 December 1920. The first motor cars were not delivered until 30 January 1921, entering service on 14 February. Although regarded as not being compatible with earlier District Railway stock, it may be assumed that certainly trailer cars must have been used with older District motors cars, if only for a short period of time and maybe only for test runs, and photographic evidence exists to suggest this.

Being of all steel construction, other features of the stock included elliptical car roofs which superseded the clerestory design, in which were incorporated six large ventilators. These soon fell into disuse as they were draughty and caused passenger discomfort and were sealed. Passenger doors were hand-operated. Acceleration on the F stock was by hand-notching of the master controller. The F class was the last 'surface' stock to be provided with barriers between cars. Hitherto, pantograph 'gates' were provided, but the F stock had leather-covered chains between cars. They later fell into disuse and were removed. With 12 motors (two sets of two motors on three DM cars in each train), the F stock was far superior to its predecessors and allowed excessive speeds to be attained, but this superiority placed strains on substation equipment. Nevertheless, the F stock was very useful for operating the non-stopping services on the District, along with clearing football crowds at West Ham and Fulham. Fairly soon, however, 15 DMs (625–639) each had one set of equipment removed, 14 sets of which were used to re-equip the seven District Railway electric locomotives between 1925 and 1928, then in use on the Ealing – Southend service as far as Barking. Two of the newly single-equipped motor cars faced west, while 13 faced east. There were only ten double-equipped motors that faced west and an error in train make-up could mean that a train could be either over- or underpowered. The opportunity was also taken to remove the second driving cab on all motor cars.

An eight-car train of F stock approaches Barking on 5 August 1950, before transfer to the Metropolitan Line. *John H. Meredith*

The rear of an F stock train on the Metropolitan Line at Harrow-on-the-Hill. One of the improvements made under the 1950s rehabilitation programme was to fit windscreen wipers to this stock. *F.G. Reynolds*

Originally, the F stock was extremely versatile with control and bus line jumpers duplicated on each side of the headstock. Any formation could thus be operated and cars could face any direction. When new, the Westinghouse air brake was fitted, but even so, the F stock was not compatible with the earlier District Railway stock. Despite the success of the F stock, the interiors were soon regarded as cold and unfriendly. To overcome this, the roof ventilators were sealed and the leather upholstery replaced by moquette. The interiors were repainted green and cream and the vertical grab poles were replaced by straps hung on horizontal poles above head height.

F stock trains were formed as follows: M – 3T – 1/3T – 3T – M + 1/3CT – 3T – M. In 1928 an F stock train was experimentally fitted with electro-pneumatic brakes, following which, all the stock was subsequently fitted. This reduced the flexibility of the F stock, as the control jumper on one side of the car was needed for the e.p. brake wires, the other side being used for traction control. Between 1927 and 1929, driving motor cars were renumbered in the 7xx series (760–799), while control trailers numbered 9xx became 19xx (all in numerical sequence). A second renumbering of many DM and CT cars took place in 1929–30, to distinguish between westbound ('A'-end) and eastbound ('D'-end) facing cars, which the previous numbering system did not do. This gave the following number allocations:

Type of Car	Total	Numbers	
DM double-equipped 'A'-end West	12*	776–798	Even
DM double-equipped 'D'-end East	13	775–799	Odd
DM single-equipped 'D'-end East	15	745–773	Odd
CT 'A'-end West	12	1900–1922	Even

Note * Two double-equipped 'East' DMs converted to 'West' DMs.

It will be appreciated that the second renumbering scheme did not keep the cars identified in original order – they were in the order of their particular type (i.e. east/west facing, single/double equipped). Trailers were renumbered in 1927–30 in sequence (composite cars 1000 – 1011 to 1588 – 1599 and 3rd class cars 1100 – 1135 to 1664 – 1699) and did not have to be renumbered a second time.

Following this renumbering, out of the 100 cars available, 12x8-car trains could be formed, with four motor coaches spare. Each eight-car train was thus formed:

D/E	S/E	D/E
'A' DM – 3T – 1/3T – 3T –	'D' DM + 'A' 1/3 CT – 3T –	'D' DM

Trains were split at Acton Town and the apparent unequal portions of the train formation (one three-car and one five-car) was to allow the longer portion to serve Ealing Broadway, while the three-car portion went to Hounslow or South Harrow. The western extensions to the Piccadilly Line in 1932 saw the end of this.

In common with most other London Transport passenger rolling stock at the time, the F stock was renumbered in a scheme that was devised in 1930. Although some new tube cars received numbers in the new series in 1931, much renumbering was done after the formation of the LPTB. The F stock received its new numbers in June and July 1935 with motor coaches being renumbered 46xx, control trailers 60xx and trailers 8xx.

The 1935–40 New Works Programme affected all London Underground rolling stock in some form or another, to a greater or lesser degree, be its designation for scrap or its updating and modernisation. For the F stock, then less than two decades old, it was decided that it should be renovated. The work included:

- Converting the hand-operated passenger doors to air operation.

- Fitting passenger door control.

- Convert the 12 control trailers to single-equipped motor cars.

- Remove the non-stop indicators from the motor car sides.

- The e.p. brake equipment to be fitted with mercury retarders.

The equipment for the control trailer to motor conversion came from the District Railway electric locomotives, which were withdrawn in September 1939 when the Ealing – Southend service was curtailed just after the outbreak of the Second World War. These locomotives had been re-equipped with then spare F stock equipment in 1925–28 and it was now returning to its original owner! The situation, however, allowed train formations to be changed from the 5+3 configuration to 4+4 but there were only 12 control trailers to convert, although there were 15 existing single-equipped motor cars. To even up the situation, further conversions were undertaken, with one single-equipped 'D' DM car (4609) turned and converted, a double-equipped 'A' DM car (4616), and existing single-equipped 'D' DM car 4619 turned and converted to an 'A' car (4618). With the even 4+4 formations, 12 3rd class trailers were converted to composite cars, making 24 of each type, being given partitions and first class upholstery from the control trailer cars.

The situation can therefore be summarised thus:

		Before	*After*	*Net changes*
Double-equipped	'West' DMs	12	13	+1
Double-equipped	'East' DMs	13	13	
Single-equipped	'West' DMs	–	13	+13
Single-equipped	'East' DMs	15	13	–2
	'West' CTs	12	–	–12
	1st/3rd Trailers	12	24	+12
	3rd class Trailers	36	24	–12
Total Stock:		**100**	**100**	

On all single-equipped motor cars, the guard's controls were removed, restricting their use to the middle of trains. The former double-equipped motor cars converted to single-equipped motors were always recognisable by retaining the rain strip (over a saloon window!) at the trailing end, where the second cab used to be, while the single-equipped DMs that were ex-control trailers never had a rain strip there anyway. The first 'modernised' train of F stock to run on the District in the revised formation with air-operated doors did so on 15 August 1938, although work on the stock as a whole was not finished until April 1940. The F stock train formations were then as follows:

D/E	S/E	S/E*		D/E
'A' DM – 3T – 1/3T – 'D' DM	+	'A' DM – 3T – 1/3T – 'D' DM

Note * Former control trailer cars (except for 4618).

The altered first class accommodation arrangements were short-lived, as the Second World War led to its abandonment from 1 February 1940. Similarly, passenger door control was soon taken out of use because it was difficult to operate in 'blackout' conditions, although it was reinstated in the 1950s. Although numerous Underground cars were damaged during the war, only a small handful were actually written off. This included one F stock single-equipped motor car 4636 (an ex-control trailer) which was destroyed at Parsons Green on 9 September 1940 and officially scrapped on 24 April 1941. It was beyond repair and as nothing else was akin to the F stock, nothing directly replaced it and the fleet continued to work one car short.

The F stock was again the subject of attention in 1949–50 and became involved in the Circle stock replacement and new R stock programme. The ideal situation would have been to replace the 90 cars of Circle stock with the 99 cars of F stock, but because of the latter's inflexible eight-car formations (the Circle operated five-car trains, later increased to six cars), a series of complex stock 'cascades' applied instead. Summarising, the various rolling stock moves were:

- New R stock to the District Line.
- District C, D and E stock withdrawn (except for the East London and Olympia shuttle cars).
- District F stock to the Metropolitan Line.
- (Some) P stock from the Metropolitan Line to the Circle Line.
- Old Circle stock withdrawn and scrapped.

The F stock on the Metropolitan Line was in fact used mostly on the Uxbridge service (the first in September 1950), for which it was ideal, being fast and capable of loading large numbers of passengers quickly. In this latter respect, it was particularly useful for clearing crowds during special events at Wembley.

At the time of transfer from the District to the Metropolitan Line, the opportunity was taken to further update and improve the F stock, to give it a further ten years life before its eventual replacement. Work included:

- Renewing cabling.
- Replacement of steel-sheeted wooden doors with new doors cast in aluminium alloy.
- Replacement of corroded side panels.
- Removal of (disused) non-stop indicators from trailer car sides.
- Additional lighting and improved décor and seating.
- Replacement of the e.p. brake controllers by the standard 'A' type (which came from former control trailers converted to trailers on Pre-1938 Tube Stock).
- Fitting of electric window wipers.
- Restoration of passenger door control (q.v. above).

Transfers to Acton Works for modifications were undertaken from Neasden, as the stock had already been transferred away from the District. The first refurbished train ran in service on the Metropolitan Line in 1951, but the modernisation programme took until the end of 1953 to complete.

In reality, the number of F stock trains available exceeded those required for the Metropolitan Line service, and with the District handworked-door C, D and E stock of 1910–13 vintage still at work on the East London Line, spare sets of F stock were made available to work on this short branch line. Being required to operate only in four-car formations, a special group of four-car trains had to be created for this service. With a double-equipped and single-equipped DM in each set (the latter type having no guard's control panels) the guard always had to perform his duties from the former, even if it was at the leading position. Also, special arrangements were necessary for battery charging. Ten four-car sets were dedicated for the East London Line service, although only six were required for normal service at New Cross (five in service and one spare). Based at Neasden for maintenance purposes, F stock took over from District C, D and E stock (which had been based at Ealing Common) from 7 December 1953, continuing a tradition maintained to this day that the East London Line has second-hand rolling stock of whatever type happens to be conveniently available at the time.

Interior of F stock after final refurbishment in 1952 for Metropolitan Line service. The end car windows were retained on this stock, the only stock to have this feature at the time. *LT Museum*

F stock was used on the East London Line in four-car formations from December 1953, bringing air-operated door stock to the line for the first time. A train stands at New Cross Gate. *Author's collection*

DRIVING MOTOR CARS – 40

Orig. No.	1st LER Reno. ‡	2nd LER Reno. ‡	1930s No.	Equipment type	Reno.	Date
625	785	745	**4591**	Single		
616	776		**4592**	Double		
626	786	747	**4593**	Single		
600	760	778	**4594**	Double		
627	787	749	**4595**	Single		
620	780		**4596**	Double		
628	788	751	**4597**	Single		
601	761	782	**4598**	Double		
629	789	753	**4599**	Single		
602	762	784	**4600**	Double		
630	790	755	**4601**	Single		
603	763	786	**4602**	Double		
631	791	757	**4603**	Single		
604	764	788	**4604**	Double		
632	792	759	**4605**	Single		
606	766	790	**4606**	Double		
633	793	761	**4607**	Single		
608	768	792	**4608**	Double		
634	794	763	4609	Single	**4616***	12.12.38
609	769	794	**4610**	Double		
635	795	765	**4611**	Single		
613	773	796	**4612**	Double		
636	796	767	**4613**	Single		
619	779	798	**4614**	Double		
637	797	769	**4615**	Single		
638	798	771	**4617**	Single		
639	799	773	4619	Single	**4618†**	18.11.39
615	775		**4621**	Double		
617	777		**4623**	Double		
605	765	779	**4625**	Double		
621	781		**4627**	Double		
623	783		**4629**	Double		
607	767	785	**4631**	Double		
610	770	787	**4633**	Double		
611	771	789	**4635**	Double		
612	772	791	**4637**	Double		
614	774	793	**4639**	Double		
618	778	795	**4641**	Double		
622	782	797	**4643**	Double		
624	784	799	**4645**	Double		

* Turned and converted from 'D' to 'A' and converted to double-equipped car.
† Turned and converted from 'D' to 'A', remaining single-equipped.
‡ Renumbering 1928–30.

CONTROL TRAILERS – 12 (CONVERTED TO SINGLE-EQUIPPED DRIVING MOTOR CARS 1938–40)

Orig. No.	1st LER Reno. ‡	2nd LER Reno. ‡	1930s No.	DM Conversion	Date	Disposal
900	1900		6000	**4620**	17.06.39	
902	1902		6002	**4622**	28.08.39	
904	1904		6004	**4624**	23.03.40	
906	1906		6006	**4626**	15.07.38	
908	1908		6008	**4628**	30.01.39	
910	1910		6010	**4630**	06.01.40	
901	1901	1912	6012	**4632**	02.12.39	
903	1903	1914	6014	**4634**	09.09.39	
905	1905	1916	6016	**4636**	06.04.40	24.04.41
907	1907	1918	6018	**4638**	03.02.40	
909	1909	1920	6020	**4640**	01.07.39	
911	1911	1922	6022	**4642**	22.07.39	

‡ Renumbering 1928–30.

1ST/3RD CLASS COMPOSITE TRAILERS – 12

Orig. No.	LER Reno. 1928–29	1930s No.	Orig. No.	LER Reno. 1928–29	1930s No.
1000	1588	**8000**	1006	1594	**8006**
1001	1589	**8001**	1007	1595	**8007**
1002	1590	**8002**	1008	1596	**8008**
1003	1591	**8003**	1009	1597	**8009**
1004	1592	**8004**	1010	1598	**8010**
1005	1593	**8005**	1011	1599	**8011**

THIRD CLASS TRAILERS – 36

Orig. No.	LER Reno. 1928–29	1930s No.	Reno.	Date	Orig. No.	LER Reno. 1928–29	1930s No.	Reno.	Date
1100	1664	8500	**8085**	05.08.39	1118	1682	8518	**8093**	27.01.40
1101	1665	8501	**8086**	10.06.39	1119	1683	8519		
1102	1666	8502	**8089**	01.07.39	1120	1684	8520		
1103	1667	8503	**8087**	23.03.39	1121	1685	8521		
1104	1668	8504			1122	1686	8522		
1105	1669	8505	**8092**	16.12.39	1123	1687	8523	**8088**	08.07.39
1106	1670	8506			1124	1688	8524	**8090**	11.11.39
1107	1671	8507			1125	1689	8525		
1108	1672	8508			1126	1690	8526		
1109	1673	8509			1127	1691	8527		
1110	1674	8510			1128	1692	8528		
1111	1675	8511			1129	1693	8529		
1112	1676	8512			1130	1694	8530		
1113	1677	8513			1131	1695	8531	**8091**	16.12.39
1114	1678	8514			1132	1696	8532	**8084**	24.12.38
1115	1679	8515			1133	1697	8533		
1116	1680	8516			1134	1698	8534	**8094**	29.07.39
1117	1681	8517			1135	1699	8535	**8095**	29.06.38

CHAPTER FOUR

DISTRICT RAILWAY G, K, L, M AND N STOCKS

G STOCK

In the early-1920s the condition of the 1905 B stock continued to give cause for concern and additional rolling stock was the only option to enable services to be maintained. To that end, 50 new motor coaches were ordered from Gloucester, and were delivered in 1924–25. This enabled the electrical equipment from 50 wooden motor cars to be removed and fitted to the new cars. From those 50, eight were scrapped (6 A stock and 2 B stock) and 42 B stock motors were converted to trailers and reconditioned. These 42 cars were renumbered in their own series – 1400–1431 and 1600–1609 and were designated as H stock (H was the next letter available in the alphabetical series). The new motor cars differed considerably from the two previous builds (the E stock of 1914 and the F stock of 1920) in that there was a return to a clerestory roof. Unlike the B, C and D types however, the clerestory continued to the ends of the car, giving each end a 'flat' finish, and the top roof line along the body had a distinctive continuous 'lip'. The bodywork on the new cars was finished in a lighter shade of red, although the doors were painted in the then traditional darker shade of crimson. Two pairs of double handworked sliding doors were provided per side, with hinged single doors at each end for the driver (cab end) and guard (trailing end). The latter also had end windows in the same shape as the driving cab windows. The driving cabs continued to have five large headlights but four were grouped together under the offside cab window, with the fifth located above that window at the corner. The cab itself was totally enclosed and was separated from the passenger saloon. With the cab being rather narrow, the G stock acquired the nickname of 'horse boxes' which was to stick throughout the life of this type. The G stock motor cars were 49ft 2in long and 9ft 0¹⁄₁₆in wide, the bodysides reverting to being straight, unlike the F stock of 1920.

Inside the cars, lighting was improved, with shaded bulbs provided along the lower section of the roof and along the cant rail over the seats. The colour scheme was green and cream, following that on contemporary tube stock, which was also used on the reconditioned H class trailers, ex-B stock.

The G stock cars were numbered 640–679 and 800–809, the latter ten designated as 'LMS' owned. Delivery began in July 1924 and was completed in May 1925. The first cars entered service in August 1924 and continued until December 1925. In 1958–60, 14 G stock motor coaches (then Q23) were converted to trailers.

This six-car Q stock train approaching East Ham on 29 June 1950 comprises a G class motor of 1923 vintage (leading), followed by five Q38 cars.
Author's collection

G STOCK DRIVING MOTOR CARS – 50

Orig. No.	1928–30 Reno.	1930s No.	Reno.	Date	Disposal	Orig. No.	1928–30 Reno.	1930s No.	Reno.	Date	Disposal
640	230	4140	08835*	20.11.59		805	319	4165	08845*	10.01.60	
673	295	4141	4206	18.02.39		653	256	4166			
641	232	4142	08836*	15.10.59		806	321	4167			25.05.59
674	297	4143	4208	06.02.39		654	258	4168			
642	234	4144				807	323	4169	08846*	13.06.59	
675	299	4145	4210	25.02.39		655	260	4170			
643	236	4146			24.04.41	808	325	4171	08847*	06.11.59	
676	301	4147	4212	06.02.39		656	262	4172			
644	238	4148				809	327	4173	08848*	10.08.59	
677	303	4149	4218	08.02.41		657	264	4174			
645	240	4150				658	266	4176			25.05.59
678	305	4151	08837*	27.06.59		659	268	4178			
646	242	4152				660	270	4180			
679	307	4153	08838*	21.02.58		661	272	4182			
647	244	4154	08839*	26.09.58		662	274	4184			
800	309	4155	08840*	24.12.59		663	276	4186			
648	246	4156	08841*	10.12.59		664	278	4188			
801	311	4157	08842*	24.12.59		665	280	4190			
649	248	4158				666	282	4192			
802	313	4159	08843*	10.01.60		667	284	4194			
650	250	4160				668	286	4196			
803	315	4161				669	288	4198			
651	252	4162				670	290	4200			
804	317	4163	08844*	15.05.59		671	292	4202			
652	254	4164				672	294	4204			

Two G stock motor cars were converted to work singly on the Acton Town–South Acton shuttle service in 1941. At the latter 4176 reverses in the single platform, although originally the line was double-tracked.
Author's collection

The opposite end of 4176 in the shuttle platform at Acton Town, showing the single head and tail light fitted in conversion.
F.G. Reynolds

K STOCK AND 1928–30 IMPROVEMENTS

With the G stock cars in service by the end of 1925, the District Railway undertook a review of its rolling stock in 1926. Resulting from that review, it was decided to convert another 110 B stock motor cars into H stock trailers and replace them with 101 new motor cars, designated as K stock. A total of 81 of these new cars were regarded as replacements, the other 20 for service enhancements. Whilst similar to their G stock counterparts, there were a number of visible differences, summarised as follows:

- The clerestory roof sloped down at the car ends to meet an arched roof.
- The destination plates and headlights were relocated under a reduced depth offside cab window. The headlights were grouped together for the first time. Headlights not required for display were blanked off by interior shutters.
- The main car windows were rearranged to have three large windows in the centre section and one large window each adjacent to the driver's cab and guard's swing door.
- Seating was reduced to 42 per car, as against 44 on the G stock.
- The guard's position was separated from the passenger saloon by glass screens, instead of metal screens as on G stock.

The K stock were numbered 499–699 (odd numbers only). Delivery began in October 1928 and the last cars were received in July 1929. The first of the new cars entered service in November 1928, the last in January 1930.

Included in the District's improvements plan was the conversion of all the trailers of C, D and E stock of 1910–14 vintage into driving motor cars. These were distinguishable from the original motor cars of the same era by having the destination plates and headlights placed under the offside cab window, as on the K stock motors. The opportunity was also taken to update the older cars with improved decor and lighting, to match the newer cars. Of the 20 C type trailers, ten of each were converted to east and west-end motor cars. All eight D stock trailers became east-end motor cars, while the four E stock trailers, two became east end and two west end.

What remained of the 1905 B stock was relegated to the shuttle services at the western end of the District Railway, working the 'local' services between South Acton and Hounslow West/South Harrow, and Putney Bridge to Edgware Road. These cars then became known as 'local stock' although some of the trailers reconditioned by the mid-1920s continued to work main line services.

The modernisation programme was completed early in 1930 and the District Railway stock comprised the following:

Stock	Motors west end	Motors east end	Trailers	Total
B	18	19	114*	151
C	26	26	–	52
D	7	23	–	30
E	15	15	–	30
G	33	17	–	50
H (ex-B)	–	–	152	152
K	–	101	–	101
Total	**99**	**201**	**266**	**566**

* The total of 114 B stock trailers comprised 96 cars reconditioned in the period 1920–25 along with 18 control trailers.

To the above totals must be added the 100 cars of non-compatible F stock, which continued to give good service in their own right, especially during peak periods. It will also be noted that the original 420 cars of B stock had been reduced to 353 – 67 had been scrapped, along with all 14 cars of 1903 'A' stock.

K STOCK MOTOR CARS – 101

Orig. No.	1930s No.	Orig. No.	1930s No.	Disposal	Orig. No.	1930s No.	Orig. No.	1930s No.	Reno.	Date
499	4175	551	4227		603	4279	655	4331		
501	4177	553	4229		605	4281	657	4333		
503	4179	555	4231		607	4283	659	4335		
505	4181	557	4233		609	4285	661	4337		
507	4183	559	4235		611	4287	663	4339		
509	4185	561	4237		613	4289	665	4341		
511	4187	563	4239		615	4291	667	4343		
513	4189	565	4241		617	4293	669	4345		
515	4191	567	4243		619	4295	671	4347		
517	4193	569	4245		621	4297	673	4349		
519	4195	571	4247		623	4299	675	4351		
521	4197	573	4249		625	4301	677	4353		
523	4199	575	4251		627	4303	679	4355		
525	4201	577	4253		629	4305	681	4357		
527	4203	579	4255		631	4307	683	4359		
529	4205	581	4257		633	4309	685	4361		
531	4207	583	4259		635	4311	687	4363	4362	24.03.55
533	4209	585	4261		637	4313	689	4365	4364	20.01.55
535	4211	587	4263		639	4315	691	4367	4366	07.01.55
537	4213	589	4265		641	4317	693	4369	4368	19.05.55
539	4215	591	4267		643	4319	695	4371	4370	04.03.55
541	4217	593	4269		645	4321	697	4373	4372	01.04.55
543	4219	595	4271		647	4323	699	4375	4374	03.05.55
545	4221	597	4273		649	4325				
547	4223	599	4275	24.04.41	651	4327				
549	4225	601	4277		653	4329				

A former K stock motor car (Q27) is at the front of this six-car train at Wimbledon on 13 July 1954. All 101 cars of this class originally faced 'east' until seven cars were turned and converted in 1955. *J.H. Aston*

L STOCK

The last rolling stock changes to affect the District Railway before the formation of the LPTB occurred in 1932. Plans to extend the Piccadilly Line westwards from Hammersmith had been on the back burner for many years but were at last coming to fruition. Piccadilly Line services took over the District's Hounslow, South Harrow and Uxbridge services in 1932–33, leaving the District with services to Wimbledon, Richmond and Ealing Broadway and, in peak hours only, Hounslow West. At the east end of the District, the line was extended to Upminster and thus the rolling stock allocation was balanced – almost. However, an order was placed with the Union Construction and Finance Company at Feltham for eight west-end motor cars and 37 trailers, the latter enabling more B stock trailers to be scrapped.

Known as the L stock, the new cars were delivered from the end of 1931 until March 1932 and entered service between March and October 1932. They were broadly similar to the K stock of 1927 but on motor cars, the guard's door slid back into a door 'pocket' rather than be hinged to open inwards. Although air-door operation was well established at the time on tube cars, and could have been incorporated on 'surface' cars, the large numbers of these cars which would need to be converted precluded its incorporation on the L stock. Two double doors per side were provided and, on trailers, single doors at each end. In most other respects they resembled the K stock, except that seating was arranged to be 40 per car and the car windows were larger and equally spaced between doorways.

The L stock was the last to be delivered in the District Railway's then current numbering system (motor cars 700–714 even numbers and trailers 1300–1336), even though tube stock at this time arrived with numbers in the 'new' system.

The class resulted in six west-end C stock motors being turned to face east, and enabled 18 B stock and 12 H stock (ex B class) trailers to be withdrawn.

By this time, the standard District Line train formation was based on a four-car set (M-T-T-M) to which could be added one or two two-car sets (T-M) at the east end, to make a maximum of six or eight cars per train. For this reason, twice as many east end motor cars were required than west, and the stock at the formation of the LPTB in 1933 was as follows:

Stock	Motors west end	Motors east end	Trailers	Total
B	18	19	96	133
C	20	32	–	52
D	7	23	–	30
E	15	15	–	30
G	33	17	–	50
H (ex-B)	–	–	140	140
K	–	101	–	101
L	8	–	37	45
Total	**101**	**207**	**273**	**581**

The 100 cars of F stock are again excluded from the totals, which retained the then 5+3 formations until air-door conversions in 1938–40, from when two four-car sets became the norm.

L STOCK DRIVING MOTOR CARS – 8

Orig. No.	1930s No.	Trailer Conv.	Date	Orig. No.	1930s No.	Trailer Conv.	Date
700	4376	**08822**	09.10.55	708	4384	**08826**	10.02.56
702	4378	**08823**	15.10.55	710	4386	**08827**	07.04.55
704	4380	**08824**	08.12.55	712	4388	**08828**	03.05.55
706	4382	**08825**	27.08.55	714	4390	**08829**	25.03.56

L STOCK TRAILERS – 37

Orig. No.	1930s No.	Reno.	Date	Orig. No.	1930s No.	Reno.	Date	Reno.	Date
1300	8012	08012	06.12.50	1319	8031	08031	01.12.50		
1301	8013	08013	06.12.50	1320	8032	08032	07.09.50		
1302	8014	08014	15.11.50	1321	8033	08033	04.10.50		
1303	8015	08015	06.11.50	1322	8034	08034	28.10.49		
1304	8016	08016	22.12.50	1323	8035	08035	17.10.50		
1305	8017	08017	22.12.50	1324	8036	08036	22.12.50		
1306	8018	08018	06.09.49	1325	8037	8801	25.02.39	08801	27.09.50
1307	8019	08019	06.10.50	1326	8038	8802	06.05.39	08802	11.02.50
1308	8020	08020	28.08.50	1327	8039	8803	23.09.39	08803	18.02.50
1309	8021	08021	15.11.50	1328	8040	8804	28.08.39	08804	18.08.50
1310	8022	08022	27.09.50	1329	8041	8805	19.12.38	08805	14.10.50
1311	8023	08023	27.12.49	1330	8042	8806	06.02.39	08806	06.12.50
1312	8024	08024	16.08.51	1331	8043	8807	07.09.39	08807	17.10.50
1313	8025	08025	06.11.50	1332	8044	8808	18.10.41	08808	22.11.50
1314	8026	08026	21.10.49	1333	8045	8809	08.07.39	08809	27.09.50
1315	8027	08027	28.11.51	1334	8046	8810*	23.08.41	08810	17.12.49
1316	8028	08028	15.10.49	1335	8047	8811	24.12.38	08811	06.10.50
1317	8029	08029	31.01.51	1336	8048	8812	13.05.39	08812	27.09.50
1318	8030	08030	18.10.51						

* 8810 was renumbered back to 8046 on 06.09.41 and then to 8810 on 18.11.41.

The L stock motor cars were similar to their K stock counterparts, but the window arrangement was more symmetrical, and the guard's door slid back into a pocket rather than being hinged. All such cars were converted to trailers in the 1950s. DM 4378 is at the rear of an eastbound District Line train departing Chiswick Park. *John Gillham*

M & N CLASSES AND EARLY LPTB IMPROVEMENTS

The early days of the LPTB resulted in plans being made to partially integrate District and Metropolitan Railway services. The first to be implemented was the extension of the Hammersmith & City Line service to East Ham and Barking, on 30 March and 4 May 1936 respectively. For this extension four additional trains were required. It was also necessary to replace further B stock trailers and to that end, 14 motors and 14 trailers were ordered from Birmingham for the Hammersmith and City line (designated M stock), and 26 trailers for the District from Metropolitan Cammell, designated N stock. Because the new cars were required fairly urgently, they were based on a previous design (the L stock of 1931) and were thus almost identical to them. The 26 N stock trailers conformed with District tradition by having hand-operated passenger doors and therefore, they were able to work with the older District types. The M stock for the Hammersmith & City Line was formed into four six-car trains. There were five west-end motors (4392–4400, even numbers), nine east-end motors (4391–4407, odd numbers), nine composite trailers (8049–8057) and five third-class trailers (8781–8785). There were thus two motors and two trailers spare, comprising one car of each type previously described, or, one four-car set.

Air-door operation was a standard feature on tube stock – it had been since 1922. Apart from B stock motor car 37, which had been equipped with air-doors since its relegation to the South Acton shuttle service, all other 'surface' cars still had hand worked doors. The opportunity was therefore taken to equip two six-car trains of M stock, not only with air-operated doors but passenger door control, where passengers could operate door push buttons inside and out. Only the necessary doors need thus be opened at stations. Door closure continued under control of the guard, who 'isolated' the doors from passenger use between stations. The two air-door trains comprised the following cars:

DMs	4393	4394	4396	4401	4403	4405
1st/3rd class Trailers	8051	8052	8053	8056		
3rd class Trailers	8782	8785				

All 28 cars of M stock were fitted with e.p. brakes, of the type first fitted to the F stock in 1928. They were delivered between February and July 1936 and entered service between May and July 1936.

N stock trailer 08068 at West Brompton, still showing the letter N on the end of the car at the bottom corner, before becoming Q35 stock. *F.G. Reynolds*

The District Line N stock composite trailers were numbered 8058–8083 and were delivered between May and September 1936, entering service between May and November of the same year. It was, however, the last stock to be built with straight car sides and clerestory roof. By this time, all stock on the Underground had been renumbered following a plan devised in 1930, those on the District Line in the series 4xxx (motor cars), 6xxx (control trailers), and 8xxx (trailers). What remained of the unrefurbished B stock (by then 37 motors, 77 trailers and 17 control trailers) retained their previous (1928–30) numbers, for they were scheduled for early withdrawal.

M STOCK DRIVING MOTOR CARS – 14
All cars entered service on the Hammersmith & City Line

Delivered	Entered service	No.	Trailer Conv.	Date	Reno.	Date
28.02.36	04.05.36	4391	8813	12.11.49	**08813**	19.09.50
24.03.36	04.05.36	4392	04392	04.04.50	**08830**	02.01.55
28.02.36	04.05.36	4393	8814	18.02.50	**08814**	19.09.50
24.03.36	04.05.36	4394	**08831**	28.01.56		
25.03.36	04.05.36	4395	**08815**	15.04.55		
24.03.36	16.07.36	4396	**08832**	17.12.55		
25.03.36	04.05.36	4397	**08816**	12.11.54		
24.03.36	02.06.36	4398	**08833**	02.07.54		
08.04.36	04.05.36	4399	**08817**	12.06.55		
25.03.36	04.05.36	4400	**08834**	21.07.54		
07.04.36	16.07.36	4401	**08818**	29.10.54		
07.04.36	16.07.36	4403	8819	13.12.47	**08819**	12.49
14.04.36	04.05.36	4405	04405	13.10.50	**08820**	09.12.54
14.04.36	02.06.36	4407	04407	31.07.50	**08821**	21.01.55

M STOCK TRAILERS – 14
All cars entered service on the Hammersmith & City Line

Delivered	Entered service	No.	Reno.	Date	Delivered	Entered service	No.	Reno.	Date
27.04.36	04.05.36	8049	**08049**	12.07.51	18.05.36	16.07.36	8056	**08056**	26.10.50
27.04.36	04.05.36	8050	**08050**	06.11.50	18.05.36	02.06.36	8057	**08057**	10.03.52
27.04.36	04.05.36	8051	**08051**	31.01.51	08.04.36	02.06.36	8781	**08781**	15.02.51
01.05.36	16.07.36	8052	**08052**	Not known	08.04.36	04.05.36	8782	**08782**	04.10.50
01.05.36	04.05.36	8053	**08053**	17.12.49	14.04.36	04.05.36	8783	**08783**	15.01.51
01.05.36	04.05.36	8054	**08054**	26.02.52	14.04.36	04.05.36	8784	**08784**	15.01.51
01.05.36	04.05.36	8055	**08055**	10.01.52	27.07.36	16.07.36	8785	**08785**	15.01.51

N STOCK TRAILERS – 26
All cars entered service on the District Line

Delivered	Entered service	No.	Reno.	Date	Delivered	Entered service	No.	Reno.	Date
05.07.36	10.06.36	8058	**08058**	22.11.50	29.06.36	10.07.36	8071	**08071**	11.07.50
25.05.36	27.05.36	8059	**08059**	07.01.50	29.06.36	10.07.36	8072	**08072**	22.11.50
25.05.36	27.05.36	8060	**08060**	20.03.52	29.06.36	10.07.36	8073	**08073**	15.11.50
08.06.36	13.06.36	8061	**08061**	05.50	06.07.36	06.08.36	8074	**08074**	09.09.49
08.06.36	12.06.36	8062	**08062**	23.10.50	06.07.36	15.07.36	8075	**08075**	22.01.52
08.06.36	12.06.36	8063	**08063**	17.10.50	06.07.36	24.07.36	8076	**08076**	18.09.51
08.06.36	05.08.36	8064	**08064**	26.10.50	13.07.36	11.11.36	8077	**08077**	12.07.51
16.06.36	20.06.36	8065	**08065**	10.12.51	13.07.36	25.09.36	8078	**08078**	23.10.50
16.06.36	24.06.36	8066	**08066**	06.07.50	13.07.36	28.07.36	8079	**08079**	24.07.51
16.06.36	24.06.36	8067	**08067**	21.01.50	04.08.36	26.09.36	8080	**08080**	09.12.50
22.06.36	01.07.36	8068	**08068**	03.10.50	04.08.36	26.09.36	8081	**08081**	27.10.50
22.06.36	01.07.36	8069	**08069**	20.03.52	14.09.36	08.10.36	8082	**08082**	27.09.50
22.06.36	01.07.36	8070	**08070**	26.10.50	14.09.36	08.10.36	8083	**08083**	10.06.50

CHAPTER FIVE

Q STOCK AND H STOCK CHANGES

The LPTB's £40 million 1935–40 New Works Programme included new lines, electrified lines, station and rolling stock improvements – the plan was massive to say the least. The District Line featured in this plan, with the oldest cars to go for scrap, updating the newer ones to modern standards, and ordering new cars. The work on the F stock is described in that stock's chapter, always being incompatible with other District stock.

- All remaining cars of B stock would be withdrawn and scrapped.
- The C, D and E stocks of 1910–14 vintage were unsuitable for conversion to air-doors, even though they had a projected life expectancy of ten years or more. With these 112 C, D and E motor cars would work 37 L, 14 M and 26 N stock trailers, with hand-worked doors. With the demise of the B stock, it was natural for this group of stock to be collectively regarded as one H stock (H – Hand-worked door stock).
- The existing G, K, L and M stock motors would be converted to have e.p. brakes, driver-guard train telephones, passenger door control and air-doors fitted. To run with them, 183 new trailers would have to be built, along with 25 new motor coaches. The new cars became known as Q stock and those older cars modernised as Q (Converted). Very soon the new cars became Q38 stock whilst the existing motor cars became Q23 (ex-G class), Q27 (K), Q31 (L) and Q35 (M and N).

It will be noted that these plans included the M stock which had entered service on the Hammersmith and City Line. After that line got its new stock (the O stock q.v.), the M stock was transferred to the District. The 12 cars with air-doors were converted to hand-door operation to run with the 1910–14 motor cars.

It was decided that the East London and Addison Road Shuttles should be provided by the 1910–14 stock and a number of conversions were made from the 112 strong fleet (52 C, 30 D and 30 E), along with downgrading of twelve L stock trailers from composite to 3rd class. Two C stock motors were converted from west-end to east, eight were converted to control trailers (four east-end and four west-end), and six to 3rd class trailers. To ensure that the correct number of motor cars faced west and east, four G class motors were turned from east to west.

A line-up of new Q38 stock at the Gloucester Carriage & Wagon Co. works before delivery to London Transport. Note that the cars are fitted with passenger door push buttons and non-stop indicators. *Copeland Collection of HMRS*

The new cars of Q38 stock were all built by Gloucester. Outwardly they resembled their sister cars of O and P stock which were built for the Hammersmith & City and Metropolitan Lines respectively, having the flared skirt and flared window uppers. Trailers were provided with a dummy cab door at one end, the plan being for them to be converted to motors at a later date, which in fact, to a greater extent, happened. Because they had to work with the older stock, however, the equipment had to match. Motors were numbered 4409–4437 (odds, eastbound) and 4402–4420 (evens, westbound). Because the trailers were intended for conversion at a later date, they were numbered in the main series of the O and P types, distinction being made between west- and east-facing cars (now 'A' and 'D' end respectively). They were numbered:

	'A'-end	'D'-end
3rd class Trailers	013102–013104	014101–014103
3rd class Trailers	013167–013192	014167–014192
Composite Trailers	013105–013166	014104–014166

The rolling stock summary for the District (F stock excluded) in 1940 was as follows:

Stock	Motors west end	Motors east end	CTs west end	CTs east end	1st/3rd Trailers	3rd Trailers	Total
Handworked-door Stock:							
C	12	25	4	4	–	6	51
D	7	23	–	–	–	–	30
E	15	15	–	–	–	–	30
L	–	–	–	–	25	12	37
M	–	–	–	–	9	5	14
N	–	–	–	–	26	–	26
Total	**34**	**63**	**4**	**4**	**60**	**23**	**188**
Air-door Stock:							
Q23 (G)	37	13	–	–	–	–	50
Q27 (K)	–	101	–	–	–	–	101
Q31 (L)	8	–	–	–	–	–	8
Q35 (M)	5	9	–	–	–	–	14
Q38	10	15	–	–	125	58	208
Total	**60**	**138**	**–**	**–**	**125**	**58**	**381**

It will be noted that there is one car of C stock fewer – 4028 was scrapped as a result of a collision at Charing Cross on 17 May 1938 between a District and Circle train, after a signal wiring fault.

The Q38 trailers began delivery in October 1938 and commenced operation with the Q-converted motor cars on 14 November 1938. The first of the Q38 motor cars arrived in January 1939 and the first of these entered service on the Metropolitan Line (with Q38 trailers) from 27 March 1939. By July 1939 there were six eight-car trains in service on the Metropolitan Line, with one spare motor car. With the arrival of the Metadyne P stock on the Metropolitan, the Q38 trains were transferred to the District Line during October and November 1939, save for the spare motor car, which was transferred in May 1940. Meanwhile, the last of the Q38 trailers arrived in December 1940 with the last entering service on the District Line in March 1941.

As planned, much of the B stock was withdrawn when the new and converted Q stock cars entered service from 1938. Whilst most of it was scrapped, four motor cars and 25 trailers were stored at the outbreak of the Second World War because of the Government's decision not to scrap withdrawn rolling stock.

The double-ended motor coach for the South Acton Shuttle, No.37, continued in service until 1941, when it was replaced by two G stock motors, 4167 and 4176. Both were converted to double-ended vehicles for use singly on the branch (one in service and one spare). Only a motorman was required to operate the train, equipment being provided in each cab for door control. These two cars were no longer Q23 motors but were noted in the record books as G(23) cars. The additional cab-end was distinguishable by having one small headlight above a small tail light just above solebar level on the left hand side, instead of the five large headlights and shutters. The original B stock car, however, survived in stock until 1948.

A total of 11 District Line cars were damaged beyond repair in the early years of the Second World War. One was an F stock motor coach, dealt with separately in the F stock chapter, the other ten comprising two C stock cars (4041 and 8794), two D stock motors (4064 and 4097), one Q23 motor (4146), one H stock trailer (8210), one Q27 motor (4275) and three Q38 stock trailers (013167, 014127 and 014183). To part compensate, Q23 motor car 4149 was converted to a westbound car and renumbered 4218. The lesser damaged (trailing) end of Q38 trailer 013167 was utilised to repair damaged P stock motor 14233. The cars were not directly replaced – at least for the immediate future. It was not until the advent of the R stock (q.v.) that additional cars could be ordered to replace war damaged losses.

Even before the end of hostilities, plans were being drawn up by London Transport to withdraw the 1910–14 H stock and replace it with what was to be R stock. To that end equipment experiments were already taking place on existing rolling stock, and Q35 trailer 8784 was fitted with fluorescent lights in 1944. Less of a success was the fitting of L stock motor car 4384 with 'pull open and power close' doors. This system was successfully in operation on the Paris Métro but was not adopted on the Underground. Indeed, it is believed the car never carried passengers in this form.

An eight-car train of Q stock was fitted with outside door indicator lights in 1948, in a diamond-shaped housing on the car sides near roof level. The same train formation (4200–013144–013147–4159+013112–4165+014118–4161) was also fitted with equipment for centre guard control. The guard travelled on car 013112 and had two sets of door controls, one for each half of the train. Whilst the outside door indicator lights were standard on the new R stock to follow, centre guard operation was not pursued, apart from a short trial on the Piccadilly Line.

An eight-car all-motor car Q23 train also made a brief foray to the Metropolitan Line in June 1948, as a test on all-motor-car train operation.

In addition, it was also considered desirable to withdraw the Metropolitan's hand-worked door trains on the Circle Line, and new rolling stock orders were to reflect this. The simplest solution would have been to transfer the 99 cars of F stock to the Circle Line but it would have been difficult to form the five-car trains necessary for this service using that type of train. Therefore, the plan was amended so that the F stock went from the District to the Metropolitan and the Circle Line had P stock from the latter. The R stock programme was protracted because of austerity measures in force in early post-war Britain. It was also complex, for it involved further reorganisation of the District's rolling stock. First and foremost was the conversion of many of the Q38 trailers into motor cars, a purpose for which they had been built some ten years previously. The despatch of these cars to Gloucester for conversion thus left a deficiency of trailer cars on the District Line. The first stage of the R stock programme required 82 Q38 trailers to be converted to motors. Their place was taken by 77 L, M and N stock trailers that were converted to have e.p. brakes and air-operated doors, along with six M stock motors, but three of them had their equipment isolated to run also as trailers. The former were given an '0' prefix in their 8xxx numbering system, while three M stock motors kept their 4xxx numbers, but were also prefixed by '0'.

The introduction of the R stock enabled the first of the 1910–14 C, D and E stock cars to be withdrawn, but ten motors of this class were converted to trailers in 1950–51 to partially compensate for the conversion of the L, M and N stock trailers to Q stock. The L stock became Q31, the M and N stocks Q35.

The stage II R stock programme required another 43 trailers of Q38 stock for conversion to motors. This shortfall was made up by the conversion of further L, M and N trailers to air-door operation and were fitted with e.p. brakes. It also enabled much of the remainder of the C, D and E stock to be withdrawn. This included those running on the East London Line, for the 99 cars of F stock that was at the same time transferred to the Metropolitan Line were far in excess of what was required – a dedicated fleet of four-car sets of F stock thus replaced the H stock on the East London from 7 December 1953. There remained, however, ten cars of 1910–14 stock, which operated on the Earl's Court – Kensington Olympia shuttle service during times of exhibitions at the latter.

The last round of changes to affect the District Line's stock occurred in 1954–55 after the R stock had finished entering service. The conversion of Q38 trailers to R stock motor cars left an imbalance of Q stock motors and trailers, which was not wholly rectified with stage II of the R stock programme. The excessive number of motor cars was addressed by the conversion of the eight Q31 ex-L stock west end motors to trailers (which were renumbered 08822–08829), eight Q35 ex-M stock motors (four west end and four east end) to trailers along with the three cars temporarily adapted for use as trailers in 1950 by isolating their equipment. To ensure that there were the correct number of motor cars facing in the appropriate direction for train composition purposes, seven Q27 motor cars of ex-K stock (all of which faced east) were converted to face west – 4363–4375 (odd numbers) were renumbered respectively 4362–4374 (even numbers).

The District Line's Q stock allocation in 1955 was as follows:

Stock	Motors west end	Motors east end	Trailers	Total
Q23 (ex-G)	36	11	–	47
Q27 (ex-K)	7	93	–	100
Q31 (ex-L)	–	–	45	45
Q35 (ex-M)	–	–	28	28
Q35 (ex-N)	–	–	26	26
Q38	10	15	55	80
Total	**53**	**119**	**154**	**326**

The District Line had, of course, its new R stock, the ten cars of H stock retained for the Olympia shuttle and the two double-ended cars of G(23) stock for the South Acton shuttle. It was decided that the 30-year-old (plus) trains of H stock were unsuitable for the Olympia exhibition service and Q and R stock took over the service, the remaining H stock trains being withdrawn during February and March 1958. The ultimate replacement for the H stock came with additional R stock (2x6 car and 1x8 car), which took seven further Q38 trailers for conversion into R38/3 motor cars. In addition, 17 Q38 trailers were converted to COP trailers to lengthen Circle Line trains from five to six cars, while 14 Q23 trailers were converted from motor cars to trailers.

On 28 February 1959 the South Acton branch service was closed and the two double-ended G(23) motor cars were withdrawn and scrapped.

Q38 STOCK DRIVING MOTOR CARS – 25
All entered service on the Metropolitan Line

Delivered	Entered service	No.	Delivered	Entered service	No.	Delivered	Entered service	No.
20.01.39	22.06.39	4402	10.03.39	04.07.39	4414	08.04.39	07.06.39	4425
27.01.39	27.03.39	4404	10.03.39	24.05.39	4415	21.04.39	22.06.39	4427
03.02.39	27.03.39	4406	24.03.39	04.07.39	4416	28.04.39	07.06.39	4429
10.02.39	07.06.39	4408	18.03.39	14.04.39	4417	04.05.39	04.07.39	4431
17.02.39	27.03.39	4409	31.03.39	24.05.39	4418	12.05.39	22.06.39	4433
24.02.39	14.04.39	4410	24.03.39	24.05.39	4419	12.05.39	22.06.39	4435
24.02.39	27.03.39	4411	21.04.39	25.07.39	4420	19.05.39	04.07.39	4437
03.03.39	14.04.39	4412	31.03.39	24.05.39	4421			
03.03.39	14.04.39	4413	08.04.39	07.06.39	4423			

Q38 STOCK 'A'-END 3RD CLASS TRAILERS – 29

Delivered	Entered service	Line	No.	Disposal	Delivered	Entered service	Line	No.	
14.10.38	08.12.38	D	013102	*	03.11.39	26.03.40	D	013179	†
21.10.38	14.11.38	D	013103	*	08.12.39	18.03.40	D	013180	*
27.10.38	14.11.38	D	013104	*	23.02.40	28.05.40	D	013181	
21.10.38	14.11.38	D	013167	24.04.41	13.03.40	05.07.40	D	013182	†
27.10.38	14.11.38	D	013168	*	20.03.40	07.06.40	D	013183	*
11.11.38	20.02.39	D	013169	*	06.04.40	30.04.40	D	013184	†
18.11.38	27.02.39	D	013170	*	12.04.40	23.07.40	D	013185	†
02.12.38	25.01.39	D	013171	*	20.04.40	15.07.40	D	013186	†
09.12.38	27.03.39	M	013172	†	26.04.40	10.06.40	D	013187	†
31.12.38	17.02.39	D	013173	*	31.05.40	07.08.40	D	013188	†
10.03.39	20.03.39	D	013174	*	28.06.40	12.12.40	D	013189	*
24.03.39	14.04.39	M	013175	*	13.07.40	11.03.41	D	013190	†
08.04.39	13.04.39	D	013176	*	08.08.40	02.01.41	D	013191	†
28.04.39	05.05.39	D	013177	*	02.10.40	01.01.41	D	013192	†
04.05.39	24.05.39	M	013178	*					

Q38 STOCK 'A'-END 1ST/3RD CLASS COMPOSITE TRAILERS – 62

Delivered	Entered service	Line	No.		Delivered	Entered service	Line	No.	
27.10.38	23.11.38	D	013105	†	03.03.39	04.07.39	M	013127	
04.11.38	30.11.38	D	013106	*	18.03.39	27.04.39	D	013128	*
11.11.38	17.02.39	D	013107	*	24.03.39	14.04.39	M	013129	
18.11.38	20.03.39	D	013108	*	31.03.39	14.04.39	D	013130	*
18.11.38	20.02.39	D	013109	*	08.04.39	13.04.39	D	013131	*
25.11.38	24.12.38	D	013110	*	21.04.39	28.04.39	D	013132	
02.12.38	30.01.39	D	013111	*	28.04.39	06.06.39	D	013133	*
09.12.38	03.01.39	D	013112	*	04.05.39	07.06.39	M	013134	*
09.12.38	03.01.39	D	013113	†	12.05.39	04.07.39	M	013135	
16.12.38	25.01.39	D	013114	*	19.05.39	22.06.39	M	013136	*
31.12.38	17.02.39	D	013115	*	03.11.39	26.03.40	D	013137	*
06.01.39	17.05.39	D	013116	*	24.11.39	05.01.40	D	013138	
06.01.38	17.05.39	D	013117	*	01.12.39	07.03.40	D	013139	
06.01.39	07.06.39	M	013118	*	16.12.39	10.04.40	D	013140	†
13.01.39	24.05.39	M	013119	*	23.02.40	28.05.40	D	013141	*
13.01.39	05.05.39	D	013120	*	01.03.40	11.05.40	D	013142	*
20.01.39	06.03.39	D	013121	†	13.03.40	18.06.40	D	013143	
27.01.39	20.02.39	D	013122	*	13.03.40	10.06.40	D	013144	
03.02.39	27.03.39	M	013123	*	13.03.40	10.06.40	D	013145	
10.02.39	31.03.39	D	013124	*	20.03.40	30.05.40	D	013146	
17.02.39	13.04.39	D	013125	*	06.04.40	30.04.40	D	013147	
24.02.39	28.04.39	D	013126	*	06.04.40	01.05.40	D	013148	*

Delivered	In service	Line	No.		Delivered	In service	Line	No.	
12.04.40	02.05.40	D	013149		31.05.40	07.08.40	D	013158	
20.04.40	05.07.40	D	013150		07.06.40	26.08.40	D	013159	
20.04.40	05.07.40	D	013151		28.06.40	12.12.40	D	013160	†
26.04.40	22.05.40	D	013152		13.07.40	06.01.41	D	013161	
08.05.40	18.06.40	D	013153		08.08.40	02.01.41	D	013162	*
08.05.40	27.06.40	D	013154		30.08.40	30.11.40	D	013163	*
17.05.40	15.07.40	D	013155	*	30.08.40	30.11.40	D	013164	†
17.05.40	20.08.40	D	013156		06.12.40	21.12.40	D	013165	*
31.05.40	07.08.40	D	013157		06.12.40	21.12.40	D	013166	

Q38 STOCK 'D'-END 3RD CLASS TRAILERS – 29

Delivered	In service	Line	No.		Delivered	In service	Line	No.	Disposal
14.10.38	08.12.38	D	014101	*	24.11.39	05.01.40	D	014179	*
21.10.38	14.11.38	D	014102		23.02.40	07.03.40	D	014180	*
27.10.38	14.11.38	D	014103	*	01.03.40	11.05.40	D	014181	
21.10.38	08.12.38	D	014167	*	13.03.40	18.06.40	D	014182	*
04.11.38	30.11.38	D	014168	*	20.03.40	30.05.40	D	014183	11.07.41
11.11.38	23.11.38	D	014169	*	06.04.40	01.05.40	D	014184	
25.11.38	10.12.38	D	014170	*	12.04.40	02.05.40	D	014185	*
02.12.38	09.03.39	D	014171	*	26.04.40	27.06.40	D	014186	*
16.12.38	19.01.39	D	014172	*	17.05.40	16.08.40	D	014187	*
31.12.38	02.02.39	D	014173	*	07.06.40	26.08.40	D	014188	*
20.01.39	14.02.39	D	014174	*	28.06.40	11.12.40	D	014189	*
27.01.39	14.04.39	M	014175	*	13.07.40	10.02.41	D	014190	*
10.02.39	06.03.39	D	014176	*	30.08.40	30.11.40	D	014191	*
17.02.39	27.03.39	M	014177	*	02.10.40	27.12.40	D	014192	*
19.05.39	22.06.39	M	014178	*					

Q38 STOCK 'D'-END 1ST/3RD CLASS COMPOSITE TRAILERS – 63

Delivered	In service	Line	No.		Disposal	Delivered	In service	Line	No.	
04.11.38	23.11.38	D	014104	*		19.05.39	22.06.39	M	014136	*
04.11.38	30.11.38	D	014105	*		25.05.39	04.07.39	M	014137	*
11.11.38	30.11.38	D	014106	*		17.11.39	05.01.40	D	014138	*
18.11.38	27.02.39	D	014107	*		17.11.39	26.03.40	D	014139	*
25.11.38	08.12.38	D	014108	*		01.12.39	26.04.40	D	014140	
25.11.38	03.01.39	D	014109	*		23.02.40	26.04.40	D	014141	*
02.12.38	30.01.39	D	014110	*		23.02.40	28.05.40	D	014142	*
09.12.38	25.01.39	D	014111	*		01.03.40	18.03.40	D	014143	*
16.12.38	10.01.39	D	014112	*		13.03.40	18.06.40	D	014144	*
16.12.38	10.01.39	D	014113	*		20.03.40	07.06.40	D	014145	*
31.12.38	02.02.39	D	014114	*		20.03.40	28.05.40	D	014146	*
06.01.39	17.05.39	D	014115	*		20.03.40	01.06.40	D	014147	*
06.01.39	17.05.39	D	014116	*		12.04.40	14.05.40	D	014148	*
06.01.39	07.06.39	M	014117	*		20.04.40	05.07.40	D	014149	
13.01.39	24.05.39	M	014118			26.04.40	22.05.40	D	014150	*
13.01.39	26.01.39	D	014119	*		08.05.40	27.06.40	D	014151	*
20.01.39	31.03.39	D	014120	*		08.05.40	15.07.40	D	014152	*
27.01.39	27.03.39	M	014121	*		17.05.40	20.08.40	D	014153	*
03.02.39	14.02.39	D	014122	*		31.05.40	15.07.40	D	014154	*
03.02.39	27.04.39	D	014123	*		31.05.40	16.08.40	D	014155	*
10.02.39	14.04.39	M	014124	*		31.05.40	16.08.40	D	014156	*
17.02.39	13.04.39	D	014125	*		07.06.40	04.09.40	D	014157	*
24.02.39	20.03.39	D	014126			07.06.40	04.09.40	D	014158	*
03.03.39	22.06.39	M	014127		25.06.41	28.06.40	11.12.40	D	014159	*
10.03.39	20.03.39	D	014128	*		13.07.40	16.01.41	D	014160	*
18.03.39	27.04.39	D	014129	*		08.08.40	02.01.41	D	014161	*
18.03.39	27.04.39	D	014130	*		08.08.40	02.01.41	D	014162	*
31.03.39	14.04.39	D	014131	*		30.08.40	30.11.40	D	014163	*
21.04.39	28.04.39	D	014132	*		02.10.40	12.12.40	D	014164	*
28.04.39	24.05.39	M	014133	*		06.12.40	21.12.40	D	014165	*
04.05.39	07.06.39	M	014134	*		06.12.40	20.12.40	D	014166	*
12.05.39	04.07.39	M	014135	*						

* Converted to R stock motor cars 1949–59. † Converted to COP stock trailers 1958–60.

CHAPTER SIX

THE METADYNE STOCK

Following on from the 1934 experiments on Metropolitan Railway 'Saloon' stock that the then new LPTB had undertaken with the Metropolitan Vickers Electrical Co., it was decided that the replacement stock for the Hammersmith & City Line would comprise newly-built motor cars with Metadyne equipment. In addition to the equipment trials on a six-car train of Metropolitan saloon stock, proposals were put forward for the car body design, and to that end a mock-up was built at Acton Works around the same time. Most (but not all) of both the Metropolitan and District's previous stocks comprised clerestory roofs and the new design eliminated this feature in favour of an elliptical roof. Another feature of the older trains was the hand-operated doors and footboards at car floor level. This did nothing to discourage late-coming passengers from jumping on them and trying to enter the moving train by the hand-worked doors, despite putting their own safety at risk. On the new trains, air-operated doors were to be provided, along with a flared 'skirt' at floor level, thereby eliminating this dangerous practice. The new cars were designated O stock. This was because the District Railway had given its electric stock letter identification from 'A' (1903) and in (general) sequence to 'N' (1935), and the letter 'O' was the next available in the sequence. The Metropolitan Railway, ever independent and always 'different', did not use this system for its stocks and when the LPTB absorbed its rolling stock, some were allocated letters later in the series, despite being much older then the O stock.

The order for the O stock was placed in August 1936 – the order for 58 two-car units was split equally between Birmingham and Gloucester, each company building 29 'A' and 29 'B' (later 'D') motor cars. The new cars differed from the mock-up in that car lighting was positioned at monitor rail level, rather than at two levels, and fluted shovel lamp shades were provided instead of the standard inverted 'bowl' type shades. The new shades were open at one end to direct lighting onto the advertisements. Before the new cars arrived, however, it was realised that the proposed all-motor train formations would place a strain on the traction current system. Not only would current consumption be heavy, but there was doubt that it could cope with the regenerated current during braking. It was therefore decided to dilute train formations by inserting a trailer into each two-car unit, making two three-car units per six-car train instead of three two-car.

The O stock lacked any ventilators at the car ends, as seen on the rear of a Hammersmith & City Line train departing from Moorgate.
Author's collection

Interior of O stock motor car 14018 in Ealing Common depot, probably when new. A feature of this stock was the high seat backs – the seats on P stock stopped at window sill height. Note the 'press to open' buttons. *LT Museum*

In addition to replacing the Hammersmith & City stock of 1906 vintage, it was also necessary to replace the saloon stock of similar vintage on the Metropolitan, along with some even older compartment stock cars. The next batch of new 'Metadyne' stock was designated 'P' stock and the introduction of trailer cars to the O stock affected this and subsequent orders. The first batch of P stock comprised 53 three-car units (M-T-M) to replace the Metropolitan's saloon stock, followed by an order to replace the 1898–1900 'Ashbury' stock on the Uxbridge line – this stock had been converted from steam to electric working in the period 1906–24. This latter batch of five two-car and seven three-car units of P stock was then followed by eight three-car units for the East London Line although, as events turned out, these were not to work on this line.

The introduction of trailers into the all-motor sets on the Hammersmith & City Line gave 19 two-car units spare. Therefore a total of 19 1st/3rd class (composite) trailers were ordered to make these up to three-car units for service on the Uxbridge line, which would thus have a mix of both O and P types, both of which, whilst having minor detail differences, were operationally compatible.

The driving motor cars seated 40 passengers but there were also two tip-up seats at the trailing ends. There were a number of differences, however, and these can be summarised as follows:

The O stock motor cars had high seat backs at the transverse seat positions, while the P stock and all trailer cars had seat backs to car waist level height only.

P stock motor car 13264 at Harrow-on-the-Hill. This was one of six 'A'-end P stock motors that did not have a control panel for the guard and thus did not work at the outer end of train formations. *Real Photographs Co.*

The 'A'-end O stock motors had an air intake fitted between the backs of the centre pairs of seats. Because of this these cars had no ventilators at the car ends over the communicating or front cab door, unlike the 'D'-end O stock motors, all P stock motors and all O/P trailers. None of the O stock motor cars were originally fitted with outside door 'butterfly' cocks for emergency use. Perhaps carrying on a Metropolitan Railway tradition, where the guard was located in the cab, so was he on the O stock. On P stock, however, the guard's controls were to be found at the trailing end of the passenger saloon on motor cars. Before the O stock was delivered, it was proposed to fit door-open push buttons on one door leaf between the window and rubber edge. This was changed so that a push button would be provided at the side of each door leaf. Whilst all cars were delivered as such, the O stock motor cars had the wider section for the system as originally proposed.

The design of the trailer cars was almost identical to the driving motor cars, because of the continuing ultimate wish to operate all-motor-car trains. However, in the area of what would become the cab, a pair of transverse seats were fitted, increasing seating capacity on trailer cars to 44 (plus the two tip-up seats at the trailing end). The side cab door was permanently locked. In anticipation of this later conversion to motor cars, the 013xxx ('A'-end) trailers were given stronger underframes ready to carry the Metadyne equipment. The division between first and third class accommodation on composite trailers was marked by partitions and a swing door. The division between smoking and non-smoking accommodation on some motor cars was by a glazed partition but without a door.

The O stock comprised 116 motors and 58 trailers, the P stock 146 motors and 45 trailers, making 365 cars in all. The O/P stock fleet was numbered as follows:

Stock	Builder	'A' cars	'D' cars	Total
'O' Motors	Birmingham	13000–13028	14000–14028	58
'O' Motors	Gloucester	13029–13057	14029–14058	58
'O' 3rd Trailers	Gloucester	013058–013077	014058–014076	39
'O' 1st/3rd Trailers	Gloucester	013087–013086	014077–014086	19
'P' 1st/3rd Trailers	Gloucester	013087–013101	014087–014100	29
'P' Motors	Gloucester	13193–13245	14193–14245	106
'P' Motors	Birmingham	13246–13257	14246–14257	24
'P' 1st/3rd Trailers	Birmingham	013258–013261	014258–014261	8
'P' Motors	Birmingham	13262–13269	14262–14269	16
'P' 1st/3rd Trailers	Birmingham	013270–013273	014270–014273	8

It will be noted that numbering began at 13000 ('A' cars) and 14000 ('D' cars) and was continuous until the end of the series, the only difference between the motors and trailers being an '0' prefix on the latter. The gap in the numbers listed above was for the 183 Q38 stock trailers which were numbered in the same series (013102–013192 and 014101–014192), of which more below. It was thus the intention for the motor cars in each unit to be similarly numbered (e.g. 13000–14000) and to a great extent this indeed happened. It was not possible, of course, to apply the same rule with the trailers as these numbers did not match at all in the context of unit formations. The plan, however, soon fell apart when the O stock cars displaced by trailers went to the Metropolitan Line and became mixed with P stock. Whilst identical numbered pairs of motor cars aids record keeping, the actual situation mattered not, although some DM cars did remain in numbered pairs.

Interior of a P stock motor car in April 1949, looking towards the guard's controls. The tops of the transverse seats are in line with the windows, unlike on O stock motor cars. *LT Museum*

The O and P stock was to 'surface' lines, what the 1938 stock was to 'tube' lines – a design classic. DM 13214 leads a five-car Circle Line train at High Street Kensington. *F.G. Reynolds*

It will also be noted that no first class accommodation was provided for the Hammersmith & City Line. This was because these facilities were withdrawn in March 1936. The District and Metropolitan lines continued with first class accommodation until 1 February 1940, although the Metropolitan (main line) continued with first class accommodation until 6 October 1941. The abolition of first class accommodation on the 'surface' lines was because of economies during the Second World War – the facility was never reinstated. Indeed, although the O stock trailers for the Metropolitan Line had full-height glass partitions and swing doors, the P stock (and Q38 stock – q.v.) trailers did not, indicating perhaps that first class accommodation on the Underground was not to last anyway – the war maybe hastened its end?

The first O stock unit to be delivered arrived at Ealing Common depot on 12 July 1937, where pre-service commissioning was undertaken. Despite being intended for the Hammersmith & City Line, entry into passenger service of the first four-car all-motor train was on the District Line between Putney Bridge and Edgware Road from 16 September 1937. The first (all-motor-car) trains did not enter service on the Hammersmith & City Line until 10 December 1937.

The first examples of the third class O stock trailers were delivered on 16 June 1938, the first car entering service between two motor cars on 18 July 1938. The last of these 39 vehicles, diluting the O stock motor car pairs into M-T-M formations entered service on 4 November 1938. Meanwhile, deliveries had commenced of the visually similar but incompatible Q38 cars, which were built to work with the older District Line stock.

Delivery of the P stock commenced in June 1939, the first 24 cars entering passenger service on 17 July 1939 on the Metropolitan Line, the first day of the new (but short-lived) Uxbridge – Barking through service. The new stock deliveries continued unabated until March 1940 but the last two two-car units were delayed for a year, arriving on 2 March 1941. The entry into passenger service continued at a similar rate, but because of the Second World War, and manpower and equipment shortages, this meant that the last units entered service as late as 7 June 1943.

The plans for the allocation of the O and P stock had changed even before deliveries of the first cars had begun. There were several other changes which saw a previous proposal for 8x3-car units for the East London Line abandoned. Here, past tradition prevailed and the P stock intended for it became part of a greater number of cars intended for the District, while the East London Line stock, although changing from Metropolitan to (mostly) District, ended up with the District's older cars of handworked door C, D and E stocks. It was as a result of the changes to these plans that envisaged six 'A'-end motor cars of P stock to be confined to the inner ends of units and to that end, motor cars 13264–13269 were delivered without guard's controls. The final plan envisaged the O and P stock thus:

39x3	O stock	19½x6	Hammersmith & City Line	Comprising
50x3	O & P stock	25x8	Metropolitan Line	103x3-car and
25x2	O & P stock			28x2-car units
14x3	P stock	3x8	District Line	
3x2	P stock	4x6		

However, before this plan could be fully implemented, the ravages of the Second World War took their toll. One car (14199) was destroyed at Neasden on 27 September 1940, followed by six cars destroyed in the Blitz at Moorgate on 29 December 1940 (13036, 13229, 14042, 14049, 14229 and 014080), with another at Baker Street (14263) on 10 May 1941. The resulting imbalance of cars was not finally resolved until 1951.

The annual statistics for the 'Metadyne' stock can be summarised as follows:

	As delivered					In service				
End year	DM	3/T	1/3T	Year total	Stock total	DM	3/T	1/3T	Year total	Stock total
1937	54	–	–	54	54	32	–	–	32	32
1938	62	39	19	120	174	82	39	18	139	171
1939	124	–	40	164	338	100	–	29	129	300
1940	18	–	5	23	361	34	–	13	47	347
1941	4	–	–	4	365	10	–	2	12	359
Less wartime losses scrapped in 1941	–7	–	–1	–8	357	–7	–	–1	–8	351
1942	–	–	–	–	357	–	–	2	2	353
1943	–	–	–	–	357	4	–	–	4	357
Net total:	**255**	**39**	**63**	**357**	**357**	**255**	**39**	**63**	**357**	**357**
Intended total:	**262**	**39**	**64**	**365**	**365**	**262**	**39**	**64**	**365**	**365**

Although the O and P stocks had their differences, they were operationally compatible. Because new cars were received at Ealing Common depot for commissioning, some units worked on the District Line for a brief period and even the first passenger-carrying workings were made on that line. Formed into two or three-car units, with semi-permanent bar coupling between, the outer end motor cars were fitted with automatic Wedgelock couplers, enabling the relevant train lengths to be formed. On the Hammersmith & City Line, the six-car (all-motor two-car unit) formations were reduced to four cars in slack hours, by the uncoupling of a two-car unit. When the trailers were introduced, two three-car units operated on all services – single (three-car) units with just one compressor (on the 'D'-end car) was considered an undesirable operational practice, should that compressor fail in service. The formation on the Metropolitan Line was six cars (M-T-M+M-T-M) along with some eight cars in the peaks (M-T-M+M-T-M+M-M). However, seven-car trains occasionally operated, this being made official in 1947 with two such scheduled workings.

The early post-war period saw a re-appraisal of rolling stock requirements. Insofar as the O and P stocks were concerned, the imbalance of cars through war losses had to be addressed. The stock holding was 102x3-cars and 23x2 cars, along with five spare motor cars which could perform no other useful function other than to deputise for defective or damaged cars. To eventually form 99x3 and 30x2-car units, three 'D'-end P stock trailer cars (014270 – 014272) were selected for conversion to 'D'-end motor cars, which was undertaken by Gloucester, to where the three cars were sent on 29 October 1947. Suitably converted and renumbered (14270 – 14272 respectively) they returned on 2 June 1949 (14271) and 21 April 1950 (14270 and 14272). Entry into passenger service as P stock motor cars was on 11 May 1950 (14272), 11 September 1950 (14270) and 21 January 1951 (14271). In all respects they were exactly the same as their counterparts.

The post-war rolling stock programme envisaged changes in the use of O and P stocks and centred around new stock for the District Line (the 'R' stock) and the withdrawal of the District's C, D and E classes and the Metropolitan's 'Circle' stock, all of which still had handworked doors. Insofar as the latter was concerned, P stock was to take over the Circle Line service in five-car formations (M-T-M+M-M) and the conversion of the three trailers to motor cars took in this requirement. The replacement of the old Circle stock was, however, a lengthy process, dictated by economies of every sort in austere post-war Britain. The first P stock began working on the Circle Line on 17 February 1947 but it was not until 1 January 1951 that the programme was complete. The O and P stock fleet of 357 cars then comprised:

42x3	O stock	21x6	Hammersmith & City Line	
18x3	P stock	18x5	Circle Line	Comprising
18x2	P stock			99x3-car and 30x2-car units
39x3	O & P stock	12x8	Metropolitan Line	
12x2	O & P stock	7½x6		

The reduction of P stock on the Metropolitan Line was possible because of its part replacement by F stock from the District Line. It will also be noted that the District Line no longer had a P stock allocation – apart from some early allocations between 1937 and 1942 no other official allocations were made. However, during the period up to the end of the 1940s, P stock worked on the District Line on an 'as required' basis.

As with all rolling stock at some time or other during its life, experiments are carried out from time to time, either to improve existing techniques or to try new ones for future rolling stock still 'on the drawing board'. The O and P types were no exception and also included the rebuilding of two cars, and can be summarised thus:

- O stock motor car 13008 was rebuilt with P stock type controls in 1939, following a collision at Farringdon.

- The trailing end of P stock motor car 14233 was destroyed by bomb damage in Neasden depot. Its place was taken by the trailing end of Q38 trailer 013167 whose opposite (dummy cab) end was destroyed in similar circumstances at Plaistow. The repair work was undertaken at Acton Works with 14233 becoming available for service again in September 1941.

- Not all the composite O and P stock trailers were provided with destination and non-stop indicators. Those that were had them removed from 1950, having been mostly disused for several years.

- First class partition doors were removed from composite trailers from February 1940 but the glazed partitions remained in place.

- O stock on the Hammersmith & City Line was fitted with grab poles from early-1947 in the middle of the double doorway area. This followed on from an experiment on a Q38 trailer in June 1946. However, it was realised that the poles were an obstruction and a programme of their removal began in the early-1950s.

- Passenger door control operation was withdrawn on O stock soon after its introduction into service and was not introduced on the P stock when new. It was introduced on the Metropolitan Line in November 1950 and reintroduced on the Hammersmith & City Line in November 1952. The P stock on the Circle Line never made use of this facility, because it served only the central area and had frequent stops at mostly busy stations.

- Fluorescent lighting was fitted to two-car unit 13244 – 14244 in July 1946 as a trial for the forthcoming R stock for the District Line. The unit operated in this form until May 1955. A second motor generator was fitted, which enabled a.c. current to be provided for the experimental lighting. The same unit also trialled shoegear which could be mechanically raised by a handwheel. Both experiments were incorporated as standard on the R stock from new.

- Speedometers, often an unsuccessful piece of equipment on rolling stock of the pre-war era, were removed during the 1950s from the 40 or so cars of O and P stock originally fitted, having been blanked off for a number of years. P stock motor car 14209 was given a fluid-driven speedometer as a trial for the R stock.

- The flared window toplights were taken a stage further on trailer 013089, when the bottom section of the upper window 'flare' was given a 'smooth' finish.

- Prototype R stock bogies were fitted to P stock motor cars 13268 and 14239 in June 1944, indicating that London Transport were anxious to proceed with new stock as soon as possible once hostilities were over. However, that desire was not to be fulfilled for another five years. Metalastik rubber suspension was provided on P stock motor car 14202 for ten months from September 1945.

- Side buffer pads were fitted to all outer end motor cars from 1947. Steam locomotive-hauled trains, both passenger and freight, were commonplace on the Metropolitan and District lines and it was deemed necessary for these pads to be fitted should it be necessary for a main line train to assist a disabled surface stock train or vice versa. Presumably, an embarrassing incident generated this modification with a motor car acquiring two large buffer-shaped dents to the solebar and lower cab front at some time!

- Motor car 13216 had a bodyside sheet panel replaced in unpainted aluminium, half polished and half sanded, prior to decisions being taken for unpainted R stock. This test began in August 1951 and the car ran in service to monitor wear and tear with the two finishes.

- A five-car train of O and P stock on the Circle Line had its Metadyne equipment replaced by PCM equipment at Acton Works in 1955. This trial was considered necessary because of the unreliability of the Metadyne equipment from the late-1940s. Moreover, there were restrictions on where the regenerative braking could be used – it was prohibited on the Circle and District lines and only a lower rate was permissible on the Hammersmith & City Line. BTH had provided PCM equipment on tube stock from 1935 and it was considered highly reliable. The train was formed 13197 – 013087 – 14056 + 13056 – 14197. The first digit of the motor cars was altered from '1' to '5' on conversion and the stock types reclassified from O and P stock to CO and CP stock respectively, the 'C' denoting 'converted'. Following the success of the trial, a programme was begun in September 1957 to similarly convert all the O and P stock working on the Circle Line, which was completed by December 1958.

O STOCK DRIVING MOTOR CARS

BUILT BY BIRMINGHAM – Total 58

Delivered	Entered service	Line	No.	Disposal	Delivered	Entered service	Line	No.	Disposal
20.09.37	01.11.37	D	13000		20.09.37	01.11.37	D	14000	
06.10.37	16.11.37	D	13001		06.10.37	16.11.37	D	14001	
19.10.37	16.11.37	D	13002		19.10.37	16.11.37	D	14002	
08.11.37	11.01.38	D	13003		08.11.37	11.01.38	D	14003	
16.11.37	22.12.37	HC	13004		16.11.37	22.12.37	HC	14004	
22.11.37	11.01.38	D	13005		22.11.37	11.01.38	D	14005	
29.11.37	18.02.38	HC	13006		29.11.37	18.02.38	HC	14006	
06.12.37	26.01.38	HC	13007		06.12.37	26.01.38	HC	14007	
13.12.37	09.02.38	HC	13008		13.12.37	09.02.38	HC	14008	
20.12.37	09.02.38	HC	13009		20.12.37	09.02.38	HC	14009	
29.12.37	09.02.38	HC	13010		29.12.37	09.02.38	HC	14010	
07.01.38	18.02.38	HC	13011		07.01.38	18.02.38	HC	14011	
17.01.38	09.03.38	HC	13012		17.01.38	09.03.38	HC	14012	
24.01.38	09.03.38	HC	13013		24.01.38	09.03.38	HC	14013	
31.01.38	09.03.38	HC	13014		31.01.38	09.03.38	HC	14014	
07.02.38	16.03.38	HC	13015		07.02.38	16.03.38	HC	14015	
14.02.38	24.03.38	HC	13016		14.02.38	24.03.38	HC	14016	
21.02.38	11.04.38	HC	13017		21.02.38	11.04.38	HC	14017	
28.02.38	17.06.38	HC	13018		28.02.38	17.06.38	HC	14018	
10.03.38	23.04.38	D	13019		10.03.38	23.04.38	D	14019	
10.03.38	05.05.38	HC	13020		10.03.38	05.05.38	HC	14020	
18.03.38	26.10.38	D	13021		18.03.38	26.10.38	D	14021	
25.03.38	17.06.38	HC	13022		25.03.38	17.06.38	HC	14022	
31.03.38	23.03.39	D	13023		31.03.38	23.03.39	D	14023	
08.04.38	04.10.38	HC	13024		08.04.38	04.10.38	HC	14024	
27.05.38	16.08.38	D	13025		27.05.38	16.08.38	D	14025	
20.06.38	14.09.38	HC	13026		20.06.38	14.09.38	HC	14026	
28.06.38	04.10.38	HC	13027		28.06.38	04.10.38	HC	14027	
06.07.38	04.10.38	HC	13028		06.07.38	04.10.38	HC	14028	

BUILT BY GLOUCESTER – Total 58

Delivered	Entered service	Line	No.	Disposal	Delivered	Entered service	Line	No.	Disposal
12.07.37	16.09.37	D	13029		12.07.37	16.09.37	D	14029	
17.08.37	16.09.37	D	13030		17.08.37	16.09.37	D	14030	
30.08.37	04.10.37	D	13031		30.08.37	04.10.37	D	14031	
08.09.37	04.10.37	D	13032		08.09.37	04.10.37	D	14032	
20.09.37	18.11.37	D	13033		20.09.37	18.11.37	D	14033	
01.10.37	16.11.37	D	13034		01.10.37	16.11.37	D	14034	
07.10.37	01.11.37	D	13035		07.10.37	01.11.37	D	14035	
19.10.37	10.12.37	HC	13036	25.02.41	19.10.37	10.12.37	HC	14036	
03.11.37	10.12.37	HC	13037		03.11.37	10.12.37	HC	14037	
03.11.37	22.12.37	HC	13038		03.11.37	22.12.37	HC	14038	
15.11.37	10.12.37	HC	13039		15.11.37	10.12.37	HC	14039	
15.11.37	20.12.37	HC	13040		15.11.37	20.12.37	HC	14040	
30.11.37	03.01.38	HC	13041		30.11.37	03.01.38	HC	14041	
30.11.37	11.01.38	D	13042		30.11.37	11.01.38	D	14042	25.02.41
14.12.37	26.01.38	HC	13043		14.12.37	26.01.38	HC	14043	
14.12.37	26.01.38	HC	13044		14.12.37	26.01.38	HC	14044	
03.01.38	01.03.38	HC	13045		03.01.38	01.03.38	HC	14045	
03.01.38	01.03.38	HC	13046		03.01.38	01.03.38	HC	14046	
13.01.38	30.03.38	HC	13047		13.01.38	30.03.38	HC	14047	
24.01.38	16.03.38	HC	13048		24.01.38	16.03.38	HC	14048	

02.02.38	24.03.38	HC	13049		02.02.38	24.03.38	HC	14049	25.02.41
02.02.38	24.03.38	HC	13050		02.02.38	24.03.38	HC	14050
17.02.38	30.03.38	HC	13051		17.02.38	30.03.38	HC	14051
17.02.38	19.05.38	HC	13052		17.02.38	19.05.38	HC	14052
28.02.38	23.04.38	D	13053		28.02.38	23.04.38	D	14053
18.03.38	10.05.38	D	13054		18.03.38	10.05.38	D	14054
18.03.38	11.04.38	HC	13055		18.03.38	11.04.38	HC	14055
06.05.38	01.11.38	D	13056		06.05.38	01.11.38	D	14056
23.05.38	26.10.38	D	13057		23.05.38	26.10.38	D	14057

P STOCK DRIVING MOTOR CARS

BUILT BY GLOUCESTER – Total 106

Delivered	Entered service	Line	No.	Disposal	Delivered	Entered service	Line	No.	Disposal
09.06.39	06.12.39	M	13193		09.06.39	06.12.39	M	14193	
09.06.39	17.07.39	M	13194		16.06.39	17.07.39	M	14194	
16.06.39	24.07.39	M	13195		16.06.39	24.07.39	M	14195	
23.06.39	17.07.39	M	13196		23.06.39	17.07.39	M	14196	
23.06.39	17.07.39	M	13197		23.06.39	17.07.39	M	14197	
30.06.39	17.07.39	M	13198		30.06.39	17.07.39	M	14198	
07.07.39	17.07.39	M	13199		30.06.39	17.07.39	M	14199	31.05.41
07.07.39	17.07.39	M	13200		07.07.39	17.07.39	M	14200	
14.07.39	24.07.39	M	13201		14.07.39	24.07.39	M	14201	
24.07.39	08.08.39	M	13202		14.07.39	08.08.39	M	14202	
24.07.39	08.08.39	M	13203		24.07.39	08.08.39	M	14203	
28.07.38	22.08.39	M	13204		28.07.39	22.08.39	M	14204	
04.08.39	06.09.39	M	13205		28.07.39	06.09.39	M	14205	
04.08.39	25.08.39	M	13206		04.08.39	25.08.39	M	14206	
18.08.39	13.09.39	M	13207		18.08.39	13.09.39	M	14207	
25.08.39	13.09.39	M	13208		18.08.39	13.09.39	M	14208	
25.09.39	25.09.39	M	13209		25.08.39	25.09.39	M	14209	
01.09.39	16.10.39	M	13210		01.09.39	16.10.39	M	14210	
08.09.39	03.10.39	M	13211		01.09.39	03.10.39	M	14211	
08.09.39	24.10.39	M	13212		08.09.39	24.10.39	M	14212	
15.09.39	03.10.39	M	13213		15.09.39	03.10.39	M	14213	
23.09.39	18.10.39	M	13214		15.09.39	18.10.39	M	14214	
23.09.39	18.10.39	M	13215		23.09.39	18.10.39	M	14215	
29.09.39	24.10.39	M	13216		29.09.39	24.10.39	M	14216	
13.10.39	10.11.39	M	13217		29.09.39	10.11.39	M	14217	
13.10.39	31.10.39	M	13218		13.10.39	31.10.39	M	14218	
27.10.39	29.11.39	M	13219		13.10.39	29.11.39	M	14219	
27.10.39	29.11.39	M	13220		27.10.39	29.11.39	M	14220	
03.11.39	06.12.39	M	13221		27.10.39	06.12.39	M	14221	
10.11.39	27.01.40	M	13222		27.10.39	27.01.40	M	14222	
17.11.39	23.02.40	M	13223		03.11.39	23.02.40	M	14223	
17.11.39	27.01.40	M	13224		10.11.39	27.01.40	M	14224	
17.11.39	06.02.41	M	13225		10.11.39	06.02.41	M	14225	
24.11.39	05.03.40	M	13226		17.11.39	05.03.40	M	14226	
24.11.39	07.03.40	M	13227		24.11.39	07.03.40	M	14227	
01.12.39	06.05.40	M	13228		24.11.39	06.05.40	M	14228	
01.12.39	23.01.40	M	13229	25.02.41	01.12.39	23.01.40	M	14229	25.02.41
08.12.39	29.02.40	M	13230		01.12.39	29.02.40	M	14230	
16.12.39	23.02.40	M	13231		08.12.39	23.02.40	M	14231	
16.12.39	06.02.41	M	13232		08.12.39	06.02.41	M	14232	
16.12.39	24.07.40	M	13233		16.12.39	24.07.40	M	14233	
22.12.39	13.02.40	M	13234		22.12.39	13.02.40	M	14234	
04.01.40	06.05.40	M	13235		04.01.40	06.05.40	M	14235	

04.01.40	23.02.40	M	13236		04.01.40	23.02.40	M	14236
12.01.40	13.03.41	D	13237		12.01.40	13.03.41	D	14237
19.01.40	06.02.41	M	13238		19.01.40	06.02.41	M	14238
19.01.40	28.08.40	M	13239		27.01.40	28.08.40	M	14239
27.01.40	24.04.40	M	13240		27.01.40	24.04.40	M	14240
10.02.40	13.03.41	D	13241		16.02.40	13.03.41	D	14241
16.02.40	28.08.40	M	13242		16.02.40	28.08.40	M	14242
01.03.40	24.04.40	M	13243		01.03.40	24.04.40	M	14243
21.03.41	07.06.43	M	13244		21.03.41	07.06.43	M	14244
21.03.41	07.06.43	M	13245		21.03.41	07.06.43	M	14245

BUILT BY BIRMINGHAM – Total 40

Delivered	Entered service	Line	No.	Disposal	Delivered	Entered service	Line	No.	Disposal
05.06.39	17.07.39	M	13246		05.06.39	17.07.39	M	14246	
12.06.39	17.07.39	M	13247		12.06.39	17.07.39	M	14247	
12.06.39	17.07.39	M	13248		12.06.39	17.07.39	M	14248	
20.06.39	01.08.39	M	13249		20.06.39	01.08.39	M	14249	
20.06.39	25.08.39	M	13250		20.06.39	25.08.39	M	14250	
27.06.39	17.07.39	M	13251		27.06.39	17.07.39	M	14251	
27.06.39	17.07.39	M	13252		27.06.39	17.07.39	M	14252	
04.07.39	01.08.39	M	13253		04.07.39	01.08.39	M	14253	
04.07.39	24.07.39	M	13254		04.07.39	24.07.39	M	14254	
10.07.39	19.08.39	M	13255		10.07.39	19.08.39	M	14255	
17.07.39	25.08.39	M	13256		17.07.39	25.08.39	M	14256	
25.07.39	04.10.39	M	13257		25.07.39	04.10.39	M	14257	
31.07.39	06.09.39	M	13262		31.07.39	06.09.39	M	14262	
08.08.39	13.09.39	M	13263		08.08.39	13.09.39	M	14263	30.08.41
21.08.39	29.09.39	M	13264		21.08.39	29.09.39	M	14264	
29.08.39	25.09.39	M	13265		29.08.39	25.09.39	M	14265	
29.08.39	29.09.39	M	13266		29.08.39	29.09.39	M	14266	
09.09.39	29.09.39	M	13267		09.09.39	29.09.39	M	14267	
18.09.39	03.10.39	M	13268		18.09.39	03.10.39	M	14268	
02.10.39	24.10.39	M	13269		02.10.39	24.10.39	M	14269	

O STOCK 3RD CLASS TRAILERS

BUILT BY GLOUCESTER – Total 39

Delivered	Entered service	Line	No.	Disposal	Delivered	Entered service	Line	No.	Disposal
16.06.38	03.08.38	HC	013058		16.06.38	27.08.39	HC	014058	
16.06.38	20.07.38	HC	013059		29.06.38	03.09.38	HC	014059	
29.06.38	06.09.38	HC	013060		29.06.38	03.10.38	HC	014060	
08.07.38	18.07.38	HC	013061		08.07.38	18.07.38	HC	014061	
18.07.38	26.07.38	HC	013062		08.07.38	03.08.38	HC	014062	
18.07.38	26.07.38	HC	013063		18.07.38	13.08.38	HC	014063	
28.07.38	20.08.38	HC	013064		28.07.38	26.08.38	HC	014064	
12.08.38	10.09.38	HC	013065		12.08.38	14.09.38	HC	014065	
12.08.38	03.10.38	HC	013066		12.08.38	10.09.38	HC	014066	
22.08.38	06.09.38	HC	013067		22.08.38	03.09.38	HC	014067	
26.08.38	20.09.38	HC	013068		26.08.38	21.09.38	HC	014068	
02.09.38	09.09.38	HC	013069		02.09.38	09.09.38	HC	014069	
09.09.38	15.09.38	HC	013070		09.09.38	15.09.38	HC	014070	
09.09.38	15.09.38	HC	013071		09.09.38	20.09.38	HC	014071	
16.09.38	29.09.38	HC	013072		16.09.38	26.09.38	HC	014072	
23.09.38	29.09.38	HC	013073		23.09.38	04.10.38	HC	014073	
30.09.38	12.10.38	HC	013074		30.09.38	12.10.38	HC	014074	
30.09.38	02.11.38	D	013075		30.09.38	01.11.38	D	014075	

07.10.38	20.10.38	HC	**013076**		07.10.38	04.11.38	HC	**014076**
14.10.38	21.10.38	HC	**013077**					

O STOCK 1ST/3RD CLASS TRAILERS

BUILT BY GLOUCESTER - Total 19

Delivered	Entered service	Line	No.	Disposal	Delivered	Entered service	Line	No.	Disposal
29.06.38	20.07.38	HC	**013078**		16.06.38	14.09.38	HC	**014077**	
18.07.38	27.07.38	HC	**013079**		08.07.38	29.07.38	HC	**014078**	
28.07.38	16.08.38	HC	**013080**		28.07.38	18.08.38	HC	**014079**	
22.08.38	27.08.38	HC	**013081**		22.08.38	02.09.38	HC	**014080**	25.02.41
26.08.38	15.09.38	HC	**013082**		26.08.38	04.10.38	HC	**014081**	
02.09.38	12.09.38	HC	**013083**		02.09.38	07.09.38	HC	**014082**	
16.09.38	23.09.38	HC	**013084**		16.09.38	23.09.38	HC	**014083**	
23.09.38	07.11.38	D	**013085**		23.09.38	01.11.38	D	**014084**	
07.10.38	17.10.38	HC	**013086**		07.10.38	23.03.39	D	**014085**	
					14.10.38	02.11.38	D	**014086**	

P STOCK 1ST/3RD CLASS TRAILERS

BUILT BY GLOUCESTER – Total 29

Delivered	Entered service	Line	No.	Disposal	Delivered	Entered service	Line	No.	Disposal
25.05.39	23.02.40	M	**013087**		25.05.39	27.01.40	M	**014087**	
09.06.39	17.07.39	M	**013088**		25.05.39	29.02.40	M	**014088**	
23.06.39	24.07.39	M	**013089**		16.06.39	17.07.39	M	**014089**	
07.07.39	01.08.39	M	**013090**		30.06.39	24.07.39	M	**014090**	
24.07.39	08.08.39	M	**013091**		14.07.39	01.08.39	M	**014091**	
04.08.39	25.08.39	M	**013092**		28.07.39	06.09.39	M	**014092**	
25.08.39	25.09.39	M	**013093**		18.08.39	13.09.39	M	**014093**	
08.09.39	24.10.39	M	**013094**		01.09.39	03.10.39	M	**014094**	
23.09.39	18.10.39	M	**013095**		15.09.39	03.10.39	M	**014095**	
13.10.39	31.10.39	M	**013096**		29.09.39	24.10.39	M	**014096**	
27.10.39	06.12.39	M	**013097**		13.10.39	29.11.39	M	**014097**	
22.12.39	13.02.40	M	**013098**		03.11.39	29.11.39	M	**014098**	
12.01.40	06.08.42	M	**013099**		04.01.40	23.02.40	M	**014099**	
19.01.40	28.08.40	M	**013100**		12.01.40	06.05.40	M	**014100**	
10.02.40	06.02.41	M	**013101**						

P STOCK 1ST/3RD CLASS TRAILERS

BUILT BY BIRMINGHAM - Total 16

Delivered	Entered service	Line	No.	Disposal	Delivered	Entered service	Line	No.	Disposal
10.07.39	04.10.39	M	**013258**		10.07.39	19.08.39	M	**014258**	
17.07.39	25.08.39	M	**013259**		25.07.39	27.01.40	M	**014259**	
31.07.39	06.09.39	M	**013260**		08.08.39	13.09.39	M	**014260**	
21.08.39	29.09.39	M	**013261**		09.09.39	29.09.39	M	**014261**	
18.09.39	18.10.39	M	**013270**		02.10.39	24.04.40	M	**014270**	
02.10.39	06.02.41	M	**013271**		09.10.39	29.06.42	M	**014271**	
09.10.39	28.08.40	M	**013272**		16.10.39	24.07.40	M	**014272**	
16.10.39	06.05.40	M	**013273**		16.10.39	24.04.40	M	**014273**	

CONVERSION OF P STOCK TRAILER CARS TO DRIVING MOTOR CARS

No.	To Gloucester	Reno.	Returned	Entered service
014270	29.10.48	**14270**	21.04.49	11.09.50
014271	29.10.47	**14271**	02.06.49	21.01.51
014272	29.10.47	**14272**	21.04.49	11.05.50

CONVERSION OF DRIVING MOTOR CARS FROM METADYNE TO PCM EQUIPMENT

O STOCK

No.	P.C.M. Conv'n	Date	No.	P.C.M. Conv'n	Date
13008	**53008**	15.11.57	14040	**54040**	15.11.57
13021	**53021**	03.12.58	14041	**54041**	03.12.58
13043	**53043**	06.09.57	14043	**54043**	06.09.57
13044	**53044**	25.08.58	14044	**54044**	25.08.58
13045	**53045**	14.01.58	14045	**54045**	14.01.58
13046	**53046**	25.06.58	14046	**54046**	25.06.58
13047	**53047**	13.02.58	14047	**54047**	13.02.58
13048	**53048**	15.09.58	14048	**54048**	15.09.58
13049	**53049**	22.05.58	14051	**54051**	10.11.58
13051	**53051**	10.11.58	14053	**54053**	02.10.57
13053	**53053**	02.10.57	14054	**54054**	29.04.58
13054	**53054**	29.04.58	14055	**54055**	03.12.57
13055	**53055**	03.12.57	14056	**54056**	24.06.55
13056	**53056**	24.06.55	14057	**54057**	20.03.58
13057	**53057**	20.03.58			

P STOCK

No.	P.C.M. Conv'n	Date	No.	P.C.M. Conv'n	Date
13197	**53197**	24.06.55	14197	**54197**	24.06.55
13239	**53239**	20.02.58	14238	**54238**	22.05.58
13240	**53240**	28.10.58	14240	**54240**	28.10.58
13241	**53241**	03.12.58	14241	**54241**	03.12.58
13242	**53242**	15.11.57	14242	**54242**	15.11.57
13243	**53243**	06.09.57	14243	**54243**	06.09.57
13244	**53244**	25.08.58	14244	**54244**	25.08.58
13245	**53245**	14.01.58	14245	**54245**	14.01.58
13246	**53246**	25.06.58	14246	**54246**	25.06.58
13247	**53247**	13.02.58	14247	**54247**	13.02.58
13248	**53248**	15.09.58	14248	**54248**	15.09.58
13249	**53249**	20.02.58	14249	**54249**	20.02.58
13250	**53250**	28.10.58	14250	**54250**	28.10.58
13251	**53251**	10.11.58	14251	**54251**	10.11.58
13252	**53252**	22.05.58	14252	**54252**	22.05.58
13253	**53253**	02.10.57	14253	**54253**	02.10.57
13254	**53254**	29.04.58	14254	**54254**	29.04.58
13255	**53255**	03.12.57	14255	**54255**	03.12.57
13257	**53257**	20.03.58	14256	**54256**	20.02.58
			14257	**54257**	20.03.58

CHAPTER SEVEN

DISTRICT LINE R STOCK

The LPTB, in continuing the District Railway's policy of identifying stock by letters, had planned to use the R designation for the Metropolitan's non-Circle Line saloon stock, but as much of it was withdrawn by 1940, the letter R was not used for this purpose. It was, however, the next letter available in the series when the R stock as we know it now, was conceived.

Because of the Second World War and resulting constraints on finance and materials, the R stock story is exceedingly complex, with numerous plans, proposals and counter-proposals, as to how to utilise a limited number of new vehicles permitted by the government. Plans for new cars were first discussed in early-1942. Then it was proposed that the 107 cars of C, D and E stock of 1910–14 vintage should be replaced and new stock (6x4 cars) provided for the East London Line, making 131 in all. A re-appraisal of the East London Line's requirement to 6x3 cars reduced the proposed fleet to 125 cars by 1945. By this time the condition of the Metropolitan's Circle stock was causing concern and thoughts turned to make this the priority for replacement.

Difficulties existed in planning what to do with a relatively small number (125) of new cars. Perhaps because of an oversight, it was later realised that additional vehicles could be justified, as a direct replacement for those destroyed in the war. The figure for new stock was thus upwardly adjusted to 143 cars. Needless to say, the proposals and counter-proposals continued and it was not until the spring of 1946 that a plan was formally agreed. In short the plan was as follows:

- 18x5-car trains of P stock to be taken from the Metropolitan's Uxbridge line.
- 8x8-car trains of District F stock to replace the P stock on the Uxbridge line.
- 143 new cars of R stock to be built for the District Line.

This resulted in a surplus number of vehicles and enabled 26 cars of handworked door stock to be scrapped.

R38/1 DM 21114 leads an R stock train at West Brompton, in its early days and when fitted with the original beamless shoegear. *F.G. Reynolds*

A six-car R stock train working the Olympia shuttle service. Whilst quite similar to the O and P stock, they differed by having destination blinds at the top of the offside cab window and a separate train set number box beneath it. This, the first R stock train, was thought to have been the only one to have been fitted with 'Non-Stop' boards, as just can be seen on the leading motor car (22600).
Author's collection

It was also decided that the new cars would all be non-driving motors. To run with them, therefore, driving motor cars would be required and this enabled at least some of the 1938-built trailers to be converted to motors, which was the original intention. This, it should be noted, would see a return to all-motor-car trains.

The formation of the R stock was to be in four and two-car units, with one of each forming a six-car train, with cabs only at the outer ends. Because the District Line operated some eight-car trains at peak periods, the formation allowed another two-car unit to be added. The units were thus arranged so that the four-car units faced west and the two-car units faced east. The east end of the train is where uncoupling took place on the older stock and, if only not to increase additional costs, there was no reason to change this practice. To that end, 31x4 car and 50x2 car units were ordered, enabling 31 trains to be formed of which 19 could be eight cars.

To make this number of trains 82 trailers would be converted, 31 'A' end and 50 'D' end. These were taken from the Q38 fleet, and to compensate for their loss some 64 trailer cars from the H stock fleet were converted with air-doors and e.p. brakes in a parallel running programme. A small number of six-car P stock trains were also borrowed from the Metropolitan Line.

The order for the new non-driving motors was split between Birmingham (89 cars) and Gloucester (54 cars), the latter also undertaking the motor car conversions. It had been decided that the car numbers should not only identify the vehicle, but its type. Each six-car train therefore had six individual cars which could not be used at any other position in a train. This proved to be a nightmare during the delivery and commissioning process when the lack of a particular car type prevented complete trains being prepared for service. The proposal, therefore, that the last two numbers of each unit should be the same (e.g. 21100 – 23200 – 23300 – 23400) was soon dashed and for reasons described, all such hopes were abandoned! The 'R' stock fleet was numbered in the 2xxxx series, with the second digit indicating the type of car ('1' 'A-end' DM, '2' 'D-end' DM and '3' NDM) and the third digit (from '1' to '6') its position in a six-car train. To enable uncoupling between units, automatic Wedgelock couplers were provided at the east end of NDM car 4, the west end of NDM car 5 and the east end of DM car 6. In this way it was possible to add another 5+6 unit to a six-car train to make eight. Formations were thus:

'A' end west   *'D' end east*

Car type	DM	NDM	NDM	NDM	NDM	DM	NDM	DM
Car pos'n	1	2	3	4	5	6	5(7)	6(8)
Car No.	211xx –	232xx –	233xx –	234xx +	235xx –	226xx +	235xx –	226xx

In order that a prototype Q38 trailer to R stock motor conversion could be undertaken, Q38 trailer 014141 was sent to Gloucester on 27 November 1947. Early post war problems already mentioned delayed its completion and it was to be over another year (9 December 1948) before two other cars (013134 and 013174) were similarly despatched for conversion. Meanwhile, it had been decided that the new NDMs would be designated R47 (the '47' being the [over optimistic] anticipated year of delivery) and the converted motors cars R38. It was originally proposed to rebuild two batches of Q38 trailers into R stock motors in 'number order' (21100–21130 ex 013161–013166 and 013168–013192, 22600–22650 ex 014141–014182 and 014184–014192) but economic decisions saw the plan changed to use cars due for overhaul and those awaiting repair from minor collisions.

The new non-driving motor cars were virtually identical to each other, despite the fact there were four types. To enable uncoupling and coupling between cars 4 and 5, a key operated switch was provided at the coupling end at head height. It was provided in this form to prevent misuse by enquiring minds! The window toplights were flared gently at the top, but formed a 'diamond' shape at their ends, as tried previously on P stock trailer 013089. The centre bay contained a pair of transverse seats and three longitudinal seats either side, while the identical two ends of the cars contained five all longitudinal seats per side – total 40 per car.

The interior layout of the converted cars was changed little and continued to seat 40 passengers, with two pairs of transverse seats per side in the centre bay. Guard's controls were provided at the trailing end which were unique in having a key-operated switch (with an offset 'lug') to operate the passenger doors. Other equipment (lights, heaters, guard's doors) was provided with small trigger switches on the panel. There was even a space provided for a fan switch, but fans were never fitted. The cab front was very much like the O and P stock, but with improvements. The six headlights below the offside cab window were separated from the window by a box for train set number plates, rather than for destination plates. Separate tail lights were provided at solebar level. The offside cab window at the top incorporated a roller destination blind box. Non-stop indicators were provided only on the side of the first train, but as it had already been decided to abandon their use, no more were delivered with them. Outside door indicator lights were provided in a diamond-shaped housing, previously trialled on Q23 and Q38 stock cars in 1948. Passenger door control was provided, being introduced from May 1956. It was taken out of use in March 1959.

The first Q38 to R stock conversions were received back in November 1949 and in the same month the new R47 NDMs commenced delivery. Commissioning and crew training enabled the first eight-car train to enter service on 17 April 1950. Only seven four-car and four two-car units were formed in the proposed like-number series, and thus indicated the problems of adhering to it at an early stage. Trains continued to enter service through 1950 and into 1951, the last doing so on 11 May 1951. This was a single motor car, 22650, which was an odd vehicle provided because trains were then still ordered on a 'car' basis for spares, rather than a 'unit' basis.

By the time that the R stock began delivery at the end of 1949, further trains of R stock had been decided upon and ordered. This decision was aided by the decision to use aluminium construction because the use of steel was still very much restricted in the construction industry generally. To that end, Metro-Cammell of Birmingham was awarded the contract for 90 new cars (R stock stage II – the previous one was thus stage I) which was the balance of the number of old cars still to be scrapped. By now London Transport was thinking of its rolling stock on a 'unit' basis and thus the odd motor car from stage I was incorporated in the stage II programme. Again, the new cars were to be all non-driving motors, which would require the conversion of more Q38 stock trailers to R38 motor cars. As a result there were 84 new NDMs and six new driving motors ordered, and 43 Q38 stock trailers converted to motor cars. Taking in the spare motor car from stage I, the second stage provided 17x4-car units and 33x2-car units. All of the new cars were designated R49, with the converted motors R38. Officially, however, the motor car conversions were designated R38/1 and R38/2.

The fleet total for both stages thus amounted to 48x4-car and 83x2-car units (358 cars) giving the possibility of 35 eight-car and 13 six-car trains to be formed. However, the normal requirement was 30x8 and 12x6 with the remainder for maintenance and operational spares.

For the second stage, the first trailer-to-motor conversions were sent to Gloucester on 2 May 1951, comprising Q38 trailers 013104 and 014104. Trailer 013141, sent on 25 June 1951 was in fact the first to return (as 21131) on 24 October 1951, along with 22651 (ex–014104). Motor car 21131 was hastily pressed into service – on 27 November 1951 – with stage I NDMs. It was not until 18 January 1952 that the new NDMs arrived, the first complete stage II train entering service on 12 March 1952. Two days previously, five stage II cars had entered service with a stage I DM. A similar situation in forming up new units with cars available arose and only six of the two-car units entered service in the correct number sequence. The last R stock cars entered service on 20 March 1953.

The first new R49 NDM to be built by Metro-Cammell (23231) was chosen to be exhibited at the Festival of Britain in 1951, being the first Underground car to be constructed in aluminium alloy. For exhibition purposes, it was prepared two-thirds painted with one-third in unpainted condition.

Steel-bodied R47 NDM 23203 at West Brompton. *F.G. Reynolds*

Aluminium-bodied R49 NDM 23242 at West Brompton. The 'join' line above the doors and windows and at the car ends distinguishes this stock from the R47 type. *F.G. Reynolds*

Hitherto, new R stock had been painted in the traditional Underground train red livery, with gilt London Transport transfers beneath the centre saloon windows and gilt car numbers similarly positioned beneath the windows of each end bay. But the decision to use unpainted aluminium led London Transport to experiment with the external finishes. To that end, following on from the unpainted section of NDM 23231, it was decided to have a complete car unpainted, save for a three-inch-wide all-round red band at waist level. NDM 23567 was delivered in this form on 17 April 1952 with the car number in white on the black solebar. Subsequent problems with car identification saw the car number later applied in red beneath the centre saloon window. Passenger door open buttons were also picked out in red, compared with yellow on red-painted stock. With its red-painted DM partner (22663), the unpainted car entered service on 12 June 1952.

The success of the unpainted car, not only in technical terms but with the travelling public as well, led London Transport to having one of the eight-car trains of R49 stock (i.e. those with new motor cars rather than converted motor cars) delivered unpainted, as on NDM 23567. Naturally, the cars were delivered spasmodically from 1 October 1952. The three new motor cars (21146, 22679 and 22680) were the last to be delivered (on 31 December 1952), enabling the complete train to be formed early in 1953. Because the train was in unpainted condition, it weighed even less than a painted train built in aluminium and underwent tests before entering service to ensure that it performed equally with the other R stock trains. It entered passenger service on 19 January 1953.

When delivered, the unpainted cars had a red waistband all the way around all cars. On motor cars, however, the upper section of the red band cut into the train set number box. This was aesthetically unacceptable and after a few weeks in service the cab end bands were altered to fit below the train set number box and finish in a 'V' on the front cab door. There were thus nine unpainted R stock cars in service, NDM 23567 being the odd one out in a six or eight-car red-liveried train.

Internally, there were no differences between painted and unpainted cars but there were internal differences between the R47 and R49 batches and both R38 rebuilds. On R47 NDMs and R38/1 DMs the fluorescent lighting was arranged on the 'window' side of the handgrips, whereas on R49 and R38/2 motor cars the arrangement was reversed. Much use was made on all R stock cars of varnished wood with black lining on transverse seat backs, draught screens and the partition between the cab and saloon. Another difference between cars was that the single-leaf doors on R49 stock had rounded tops at both corners. Further, there was a 'lip' line immediately beneath the gutter line at roof level.

The success of the aluminium-built cars was borne out by the fact that a 16% weight saving was made on the newer cars which, in turn, produced savings in energy.

Other matters relating to the R stock in the period under review include the following:

- Unpainted DM 22680 was exhibited at the International Railway Congress Exhibition at Willesden in May 1954. P stock DM 13200 was also exhibited and both cars were transferred together.

- The first unpainted NDM car 23567 was exhibited at the Aluminium Development Exhibition on the South Bank in May and June 1955.

- An additional handbrake was fitted to west end 211xx DM cars in the early days to ensure that there were always three per train. This was fitted at the guard's position and was additional to that provided in the cab of these cars.

Interior of one of the later batches of R stock, whilst quite similar to the first batch, had the fluorescent lighting tubes located on the ceiling side of the hand grips, to enable easier access and maintenance. Note the black lining to the veneered wood on transverse seat backs and lower draught screens, which was soon ruined by smokers and vandalism.
LT Museum

- Four-motor equipment and a new design of bogie on DM 22682 in July 1958. Being more powerful, the motors on adjacent NDM 23580 were disconnected. It was confined to operating at the (east) end of a train and to that end had its automatic Wedgelock coupler replaced with a mechanical Ward coupler. It was tested on the Metropolitan Line, not in service, and did not return to the District Line until November 1959.

- Although the main supplier of traction equipment for the Underground had always been BTH, trials from other suppliers took place from time to time. English Electric and GEC were involved in the 1950s, the latter supplying camshaft type equipment to the seven R38/3 DMs in 1959.

- Unit 21124–23214–23314–23429 was given rubber-bonded inter-car couplings in August 1958.

- DM 22681 was fitted with experimental rubber bolster springs in May 1958.

- Dial speedometers driven from motors on DMs 21114 and 21119 from June 1958.

- Static voltage regulator on DM 22644 from January 1959.

- DM 22681 was fitted with a motor alternator and fluorescent emergency lighting in April 1959 but was removed by November 1959.

The need for additional R stock was eventually based on the requirement for 2×6-car trains for the Olympia service and 1×8 as part compensation for the Q stock. This was not without many proposals and deliberations and at one stage some new trains of R stock were once proposed for the Metropolitan Line. At the end of the day the final programme was thus:

- 20 additional cars of R stock – 7 DMs (R38/3) converted from Q38 trailers and 13 new R59 NDMs.

- 17 Q38 trailers converted to COP stock trailers, to increase Circle Line trains from five to six cars.

- 14 Q23 motor cars to be converted to trailers, to balance Q stock train formations.

The seven R38 driving motor cars were converted at Acton Works, the first pair arriving for conversion on 4 October 1959 and the last car on 4 March 1959. The new NDMs were built by Metro-Cammell in aluminium, as the previous R49 cars, but they were delivered unpainted, save for the red waistband. The driving motor cars were painted 'aluminium' with the red band and cab end 'V'. The NDMs were delivered between June and September 1959. These additional 20 cars took the fleet totals to 378 vehicles.

The numbers carried on at the end of the R49 series and were as follows:

DM	21148–21150	3
NDM	23248–23250	3
NDM	23348–23350	3
NDM	23448–23450	3
NDM	23583–23586	4
DM	22683–22686	4
		20

Underground Train File

All of the R38/3 and R59 cars had been delivered with conventional wooden shoe-beams – the original truck-mounted shoes were unsatisfactory and these too were ultimately replaced. Apart from not being fitted with passenger door push buttons (by then abandoned) the cars were almost identical to their R38/2 and R49 counterparts, but there were equipment differences. The R stock as a fleet, however, was totally compatible. None of the R38/3 and R59 cars entered service as complete trains, apart from, maybe, the last. The first (two-car) unit entered service on 7 August 1959, the last (six cars) on 26 October 1959. This may have been a complete six-car train, but could have been an eight-car (with an older two-car unit) – such detail has been lost in the mists of time.

The annual statistics for the R stock can be summarised as follows:

| | As delivered | | | | | | | In service | | | | | | |
End year	R38 DM	R49 DM	R47 NDM	R49 NDM	R59 NDM	Year total	Stock total	R38 DM	R49 DM	R47 NDM	R49 NDM	R59 NDM	Year total	Stock total
1949	6	–	16	–	–	22	22	–	–	–	–	–	–	–
1950	69	–	126	–	–	195	217	69	–	121	–	–	190	190
1951	14	–	1	–	–	15	232	14	–	22	–	–	36	226
1952	35	3	–	83	–	121	353	40	–	–	71	–	111	337
1953	1	3	–	1	–	5	358	2	6	–	13	–	21	358
1959	7	–	–	–	13	20	378	7	–	–	–	13	20	378
Total	**132**	**6**	**143**	**84**	**13**	**378**	**378**	**132**	**6**	**143**	**84**	**13**	**378**	**378**

A train of the third batch of R stock poses for the camera in Upminster depot when new in 1959. By this time, passenger door control was almost at an end and this small batch of trains was delivered without this facility. *LT Museum*

R38/1 DRIVING MOTOR CARS – 82

CONVERTED BY GLOUCESTER

'A'-END DRIVING MOTOR CARS

Orig. No.	R Stock No.	To Gloucester	Delivered	Entered service	Orig. No.	R Stock No.	To Gloucester	Delivered	Entered service
013134	21100	09.12.48	18.11.49	08.05.50	013175	21116	12.05.50	11.08.50	31.08.50
013174	21101	09.12.48	12.12.49	29.07.50	013168	21117	16.05.50	26.08.50	08.09.50
013162	21102	30.03.49	28.12.49	27.06.50	013169	21118	05.06.50	15.09.50	25.09.50
013163	21103	03.05.49	27.01.50	31.05.50	013183	21119	12.06.50	22.09.50	03.10.50
013165	21104	28.06.49	10.02.50	04.07.50	013171	21120	03.07.50	29.09.50	20.10.50
013189	21105	29.08.49	01.03.50	25.05.50	013137	21121	10.04.50	13.10.50	02.11.50
013123	21106	30.11.49	16.03.50	17.04.50	013170	21122	17.07.50	27.10.50	20.11.50
013102	21107	29.12.49	24.03.50	25.04.50	013108	21123	19.07.50	02.11.50	24.11.50
013177	21108	16.01.50	14.04.50	01.05.50	013110	21124	15.08.50	17.11.50	08.12.50
013117	21109	09.02.50	27.04.50	08.05.50	013180	21125	15.08.50	01.12.50	22.12.50
013103	21110	21.02.50	05.05.50	15.05.50	013128	21126	28.08.50	01.12.50	12.01.51
013116	21111	14.03.50	19.05.50	15.06.50	013131	21127	28.08.50	11.12.50	29.01.51
013142	21112	14.03.50	19.05.50	08.06.50	013114	21128	01.09.50	05.01.51	23.02.51
013133	21113	29.03.50	26.05.50	20.06.50	013109	21129	01.09.50	05.01.51	13.02.51
013111	21114	17.04.50	07.07.50	20.07.50	013115	21130	01.09.50	02.02.51	16.03.51
013148	21115	01.05.50	14.07.50	09.08.50					

'D'-END DRIVING MOTOR CARS

Orig. No.	R Stock No.	To Gloucester	Delivered	Entered service	Orig. No.	R Stock No.	To Gloucester	Delivered	Entered service
014141	22600	27.11.47	12.11.49	08.05.50	014176	22626	10.04.50	30.06.50	14.07.50
014147	22601	30.03.49	02.12.49	03.07.50	014168	22627	17.04.50	30.06.50	13.07.50
014189	22602	28.02.49	28.12.49	27.06.50	014172	22628	17.04.50	07.07.50	09.08.50
014151	22603	28.02.49	11.01.50	31.05.50	014180	22629	01.05.50	14.07.50	31.08.50
014160	22604	28.02.49	20.01.50	04.07.50	014130	22630	01.05.50	21.07.50	31.08.50
014182	22605	03.05.49	20.01.50	29.07.50	014114	22631	12.05.50	11.08.50	08.09.50
014192	22606	03.05.49	27.01.50	04.07.50	014111	22632	12.05.50	26.08.50	25.09.50
014158	22607	30.03.49	03.02.50	25.05.50	014169	22633	16.05.50	01.09.50	03.10.50
014162	22608	28.06.49	10.02.50	25.05.50	014109	22634	16.05.50	15.09.50	03.10.50
014152	22609	28.06.49	22.02.50	17.04.50	014129	22635	05.06.50	22.09.50	20.10.50
014150	22610	29.08.49	01.03.50	17.04.50	014108	22636	05.06.50	29.09.50	26.10.50
014142	22611	29.08.49	09.03.50	25.04.50	014155	22637	12.06.50	13.10.50	02.11.50
014188	22612	30.11.49	09.03.50	25.04.50	014125	22638	03.07.50	27.10.50	23.02.51
014159	22613	30.11.49	16.03.50	15.06.50	014103	22639	12.06.50	27.10.50	20.11.50
014163	22614	29.12.49	31.03.50	01.05.50	014171	22640	03.07.50	27.10.50	08.12.50
014166	22615	29.12.49	31.03.50	01.05.50	014110	22641	17.07.50	02.11.50	24.11.50
014165	22616	16.01.50	06.04.50	15.05.50	014107	22642	17.07.50	17.11.50	22.12.50
014179	22617	16.01.50	14.04.50	08.05.50	014106	22643	19.07.50	17.11.50	12.01.51
014164	22618	09.02.50	27.04.50	15.05.50	014121	22644	19.07.50	17.11.50	22.12.50
014153	22619	09.02.50	05.05.50	08.06.50	014105	22645	15.08.50	01.12.50	12.01.51
014190	22620	21.02.50	05.05.50	31.05.50	014178	22646	15.08.50	11.12.50	29.01.51
014156	22621	21.02.50	12.05.50	25.05.50	014120	22647	15.08.50	05.01.51	13.02.51
014191	22622	14.03.50	26.05.50	20.06.50	014123	22648	15.08.50	02.02.51	16.03.51
014167	22623	29.03.50	09.06.50	20.06.50	014113	22649	28.08.50	02.03.51	20.04.51
014170	22624	29.03.50	17.06.50	20.07.50	014177	22650	28.08.50	12.04.51	11.05.51
014173	22625	10.04.50	17.06.50	20.07.50					

R38/2 DRIVING MOTOR CARS – 43

CONVERTED BY GLOUCESTER

'A'-END DRIVING MOTOR CARS

Orig. No.	R Stock No.	To Gloucester	Delivered	Entered service	Orig. No.	R Stock No.	To Gloucester	Delivered	Entered service
013141	21131	25.06.51	24.10.51	27.11.51	013125	21139	15.04.52	24.06.52	06.08.52
013104	21132	02.05.51	15.11.51	19.03.52	013176	21140	21.04.52	21.08.52	29.08.52
013107	21133	27.08.51	18.01.52	27.03.52	013178	21141	21.04.52	04.09.52	20.09.52
013136	21134	05.11.51	07.02.52	12.03.52	013126	21142	21.04.52	11.09.52	04.10.52
013122	21135	04.12.51	15.03.52	08.04.52	013124	21143	23.06.52	06.11.52	18.11.52
013120	21136	31.12.51	03.04.52	23.04.52	013106	21144	23.06.52	04.12.52	19.12.52
013118	21137	07.01.52	24.04.52	13.05.52	013173	21145	12.05.52	19.02.53	20.03.53
013119	21138	11.02.52	15.05.52	23.05.52					

'D'-END DRIVING MOTOR CARS

Orig. No.	R Stock No.	To Gloucester	Delivered	Entered service	Orig. No.	R Stock No.	To Gloucester	Delivered	Entered service
014104	22651	02.05.51	24.10.51	19.03.52	014139	22665	24.03.52	20.06.52	12.07.52
014137	22652	25.06.51	08.11.51	27.03.52	014124	22666	24.03.52	26.06.52	30.07.52
014122	22653	25.06.51	06.12.51	12.03.52	014115	22667	24.03.52	10.07.52	24.07.52
014119	22654	25.06.51	20.12.51	27.03.52	014132	22668	15.04.52	17.07.52	14.08.52
014154	22655	27.08.51	20.12.51	08.04.52	014133	22669	15.04.52	24.07.52	26.08.52
014116	22656	27.08.51	18.01.52	10.03.52	014143	22670	15.04.52	28.08.52	10.09.52
014174	22657	05.11.51	07.02.52	08.04.52	014134	22671	12.05.52	18.09.52	04.10.52
014157	22658	04.12.51	28.02.52	30.04.52	014131	22672	12.05.52	26.09.52	17.10.52
014146	22659	04.12.51	03.04.52	23.04.52	014161	22673	02.06.52	09.10.52	30.10.52
014185	22660	23.01.52	01.05.52	13.05.52	014101	22674	02.06.52	16.10.52	07.11.52
014175	22661	23.01.52	08.05.52	23.05.52	014148	22675	02.06.52	30.10.52	18.11.52
014117	22662	03.03.52	22.05.52	03.06.52	014128	22676	02.06.52	14.11.52	29.11.52
014136	22663	03.03.52	29.05.52	12.06.52	014112	22677	23.06.52	20.11.52	10.12.52
014138	22664	17.03.52	12.06.52	26.06.52	014186	22678	23.06.52	25.12.52	04.02.53

R38/3 DRIVING MOTOR CARS – 7

CONVERTED AT ACTON WORKS

'A' END DRIVING MOTOR CARS

Orig. No.	R Stock No.	To Acton	Ex-Acton	Entered service	Orig. No.	R Stock No.	To Acton	Ex-Acton	Entered service
013130	21148	28.02.59	Oct-59	26.10.59	013155	21150	24.01.59	21.08.59	22.09.59
013112	21149	04.10.58	04.07.59	25.08.59					

'D' END DRIVING MOTOR CARS

Orig. No.	R Stock No.	To Acton	Ex-Acton	Entered service	Orig. No.	R Stock No.	To Acton	Ex-Acton	Entered service
014135	22683	16.11.58	24.06.59	07.08.59	014145	22685	21.02.59	17.09.59	22.10.59
014144	22684	04.03.59	Oct-59	26.10.59	014187	22686	04.10.58	02.06.59	15.09.59

R49 DRIVING MOTOR CARS – 6

BUILT BY METRO-CAMMELL

'A'-END DRIVING MOTOR CARS, 'D'-END DRIVING MOTOR CARS

No.	Delivered	Entered service	No.	Delivered	Entered service	No.	Delivered	Entered service
21146*	31.12.52	19.01.53	22679*	31.12.52	19.01.53	22681	07.01.53	12.02.53
21147	14.01.53	04.02.53	22680*	31.12.52	19.01.53	22682	07.01.53	04.02.53

* Delivered unpainted.

R47 NON-DRIVING MOTOR CARS – 143

NO. 2 POSITION NON-DRIVING MOTOR CARS

BUILT BY BIRMINGHAM

No.	Delivered	Entered service	No.	Delivered	Entered service	No.	Delivered	Entered service
23200	18.11.49	08.05.50	23211	23.02.50	25.04.50	23222	12.05.50	15.06.50
23201	01.12.49	29.07.50	23212	02.03.50	22.12.50	23223	18.05.50	20.06.50
23202	15.12.49	27.06.50	23213	09.03.50	01.05.50	23224	08.06.50	02.11.50
23203	15.12.49	31.05.50	23214	16.03.50	08.12.50	23225	17.06.50	20.07.50
23204	22.12.49	04.07.50	23215	23.03.50	20.11.50	23226	29.06.50	09.08.50
23205	05.01.50	25.05.50	23216	30.03.50	24.11.50	23227	28.07.50	23.08.50
23206	19.01.50	17.04.50	23217	06.04.50	08.05.50	23228	17.08.50	08.09.50
23207	26.01.50	16.03.51	23218	21.04.50	31.08.50	23229	24.08.50	25.09.50
23208	02.02.50	23.02.51	23219	21.04.50	12.01.51	23230	20.11.50	13.02.51
23209	09.02.50	20.10.50	23220	01.05.50	15.05.50			
23210	16.02.50	29.01.51	23221	05.05.50	08.06.50			

NO. 3 POSITION NON-DRIVING MOTOR CARS

BUILT BY BIRMINGHAM

No.	Delivered	Entered service	No.	Delivered	Entered service	No.	Delivered	Entered service
23300	18.11.49	08.05.50	23311	23.02.50	25.04.50	23322	18.05.50	20.06.50
23301	01.12.49	29.07.50	23312	02.03.50	12.01.51	23323	08.06.50	02.11.50
23302	15.12.49	27.06.50	23313	09.03.50	01.05.50	23324	29.06.50	09.08.50
23303	22.12.49	31.05.50	23314	16.03.50	08.12.50	23325	13.07.50	22.12.50
23304	05.01.50	04.07.50	23315	23.03.50	20.11.50	23326	28.07.50	24.11.50
23305	09.01.50	25.05.50	23316	30.03.50	20.07.50	23327	17.08.50	08.09.50
23306	19.01.50	17.04.50	23317	06.04.50	08.05.50	23328	24.08.50	25.09.50
23307	26.01.50	16.03.51	23318	21.04.50	31.08.50	23329	07.09.50	03.10.50
23308	02.02.50	23.02.51	23319	01.05.50	15.05.50	23330	20.11.50	13.02.51
23309	09.02.50	20.10.50	23320	05.05.50	08.06.50			
23310	16.02.50	29.01.51	23321	12.05.50	15.06.50			

NO. 4 POSITION NON-DRIVING MOTOR CARS

BUILT BY GLOUCESTER

No.	Delivered	Entered service	No.	Delivered	Entered service	No.	Delivered	Entered service
23400	10.11.49	08.05.50	23411	06.04.50	08.05.50	23422	01.09.50	03.10.50
23401	12.12.49	29.07.50	23412	27.04.50	15.05.50	23423	15.09.50	20.10.50
23402	11.01.50	27.06.50	23413	05.05.50	08.06.50	23424	22.09.50	08.12.50
23403	20.01.50	31.05.50	23414	12.05.50	20.11.50	23425	29.09.50	24.11.50
23404	27.01.50	04.07.50	23415	19.05.50	02.11.50	23426	13.10.50	12.01.51
23405	10.02.50	25.05.50	23416	26.05.50	20.06.50	23427	27.10.50	29.01.51
23406	22.02.50	17.04.50	23417	17.06.50	20.07.50	23428	17.11.50	23.02.51
23407	22.02.50	25.04.50	23418	30.06.50	09.08.50	23429	01.12.50	13.02.51
23408	09.03.50	01.05.50	23419	21.07.50	08.09.50	23430	06.02.51	16.03.51
23409	16.03.50	15.06.50	23420	21.07.50	31.08.50			
23410	31.03.50	22.12.50	23421	26.08.50	25.09.50			

NO. 5 POSITION NON-DRIVING MOTOR CARS
BUILT BY GLOUCESTER

No.	Delivered	Entered service	No.	Delivered	Entered service	No.	Delivered	Entered service
23500	18.11.49	08.05.50	23508	16.03.50	15.06.50	23516	17.06.50	20.07.50
23501	02.12.49	13.07.50	23509	24.03.50	29.01.51	23517	30.06.50	14.07.50
23502	28.12.49	27.06.50	23510	06.04.50	01.05.50	23518	07.07.50	09.08.50
23503	11.01.50	31.05.50	23511	14.04.50	15.05.50	23519	14.07.50	31.08.50
23504	27.01.50	04.07.50	23512	27.04.50	15.05.50	23520	11.08.50	08.09.50
23505	03.02.50	04.07.50	23513	12.05.50	25.05.50	23521	26.08.50	25.09.50
23506	22.02.50	17.04.50	23514	19.05.50	02.11.50	23522	01.09.50	03.10.50
23507	01.03.50	17.04.50	23515	09.06.50	20.06.50			

NO. 5 POSITION NON-DRIVING MOTOR CARS
BUILT BY BIRMINGHAM

No.	Delivered	Entered service	No.	Delivered	Entered service	No.	Delivered	Entered service
23523	01.12.49	25.04.50	23532	02.03.50	22.12.50	23541	12.05.50	23.02.51
23524	15.12.49	25.05.50	23533	09.03.50	01.05.50	23542	18.05.50	20.06.50
23525	09.01.50	29.07.50	23534	16.03.50	08.12.50	23543	08.06.50	03.07.50
23526	19.01.50	16.03.51	23535	23.03.50	20.11.50	23544	17.06.50	20.07.50
23527	26.01.50	20.04.51	23536	30.03.50	08.05.50	23545	29.06.50	26.10.50
23528	09.02.50	25.05.50	23537	06.04.50	31.08.50	23546	13.07.50	20.10.50
23529	09.02.50	12.01.51	23538	21.04.50	12.01.51	23547	28.07.50	22.12.50
23530	16.02.50	13.02.51	23539	01.05.50	31.05.50	23548	17.08.50	24.11.50
23531	23.02.50	25.04.50	23540	05.05.50	08.06.50	23549	07.09.50	03.10.50

R49 NON-DRIVING MOTOR CARS – 84

NO. 2 POSITION NON-DRIVING MOTOR CARS
BUILT BY METRO-CAMMELL

No.	Delivered	Entered service	No.	Delivered	Entered service	No.	Delivered	Entered service
23231	28.05.52	20.09.52	23237	27.02.52	08.04.52	23243	02.07.52	04.10.52
23232	18.01.52	10.03.52	23238	19.03.52	23.05.52	23244	17.07.52	29.08.52
23233	18.01.52	19.03.52	23239	09.04.52	13.05.52	23245	01.10.52	04.02.53
23234	13.02.52	23.04.52	23240	09.04.52	14.05.52	23246	05.11.52	19.12.52
23235	13.02.52	12.03.52	23241	05.06.52	06.08.52	23247 *	05.11.52	19.01.53
23236	27.02.52	27.03.52	23242	11.06.52	18.11.52			

NO. 3 POSITION NON-DRIVING MOTOR CARS
BUILT BY METRO-CAMMELL

No.	Delivered	Entered service	No.	Delivered	Entered service	No.	Delivered	Entered service
23331	29.01.52	19.03.52	23337	26.03.52	04.02.53	23343	11.06.52	18.11.52
23332	29.01.52	10.03.52	23338	17.04.52	19.12.52	23344	18.06.52	20.09.52
23333	13.02.52	27.03.52	23339	17.04.52	13.05.52	23345	02.07.52	04.10.52
23334	13.02.52	12.03.52	23340	07.05.52	23.05.52	23346 *	01.10.52	19.01.53
23335	05.03.52	23.04.52	23341	07.05.52	29.08.52	23347	20.11.52	20.03.53
23336	05.03.52	08.04.52	23342	21.05.52	06.08.52			

NO. 4 POSITION NON-DRIVING MOTOR CARS
BUILT BY METRO-CAMMELL

No.	Delivered	Entered service	No.	Delivered	Entered service	No.	Delivered	Entered service
23431	06.02.52	19.03.52	23437	02.04.52	08.04.52	23443	05.06.52	04.10.52
23432	06.02.52	10.03.52	23438	30.04.52	18.11.52	23444	18.06.52	20.09.52
23433	20.02.52	27.03.52	23439	30.04.52	13.05.52	23445	01.10.52	04.02.53
23434	20.02.52	12.03.52	23440	07.05.52	23.05.52	23446 *	26.11.52	19.01.53
23435	12.03.52	08.04.52	23441	13.05.52	19.12.52	23447	14.01.53	20.03.53
23436	12.03.52	23.04.52	23442	21.05.52	06.08.52			

NO. 5 POSITION NON-DRIVING MOTOR CARS
BUILT BY METRO-CAMMELL

No.	Delivered	Entered service	No.	Delivered	Entered service	No.	Delivered	Entered service
23550	18.01.52	08.04.52	23561	19.03.52	23.05.52	23572	28.05.52	10.10.52
23551	18.01.52	19.03.52	23562	26.03.52	31.10.52	23573	11.06.52	17.10.52
23552	29.01.52	27.03.52	23563	26.03.52	07.11.52	23574	02.07.52	18.11.52
23553	29.01.52	10.03.52	23564	02.04.52	10.09.52	23575	17.07.52	14.08.52
23554	06.02.52	26.06.52	23565	02.04.52	04.10.52	23576	17.07.52	30.07.52
23555	06.02.52	27.03.52	23566	09.04.52	30.04.52	23577	22.10.52	10.12.52
23556	20.02.52	12.03.52	23567	17.04.52	12.06.52	23578	22.10.52	04.02.53
23557	27.02.52	08.04.52	23568	13.05.52	26.08.52	23579	12.11.52	12.02.53
23558	05.03.52	13.05.52	23569	13.05.52	29.11.52	23580	12.11.52	04.02.53
23559	12.03.52	23.04.52	23570	21.05.52	24.07.52	23581 *	20.11.52	19.01.53
23560	19.03.52	03.06.52	23571	28.05.52	12.07.52	23582 *	26.11.52	19.01.53

* Delivered unpainted.

R59 NON-DRIVING MOTOR CARS – 13

NO. 2 POSITION NON-DRIVING MOTOR CARS, BUILT BY METRO-CAMMELL

No.	Delivered	Entered service	No.	Delivered	Entered service	No.	Delivered	Entered service
23248	29.06.59	25.08.59	23249	28.07.59	22.09.59	23250	02.09.59	26.10.59

NO. 3 POSITION NON-DRIVING MOTOR CARS, BUILT BY METRO-CAMMELL

No.	Delivered	Entered service	No.	Delivered	Entered service	No.	Delivered	Entered service
23348	29.06.59	25.08.59	23349	28.07.59	22.09.59	23350	02.09.59	26.10.59

NO. 4 POSITION NON-DRIVING MOTOR CARS, BUILT BY METRO-CAMMELL

No.	Delivered	Entered service	No.	Delivered	Entered service	No.	Delivered	Entered service
23448	29.06.59	25.08.59	23449	28.07.59	22.09.59	23450	02.09.59	26.10.59

NO. 5 POSITION NON-DRIVING MOTOR CARS, BUILT BY METRO-CAMMELL

No.	Delivered	Entered service	No.	Delivered	Entered service	No.	Delivered	Entered service
23583	29.06.59	07.08.59	23585	02.09.59	22.10.59	23586	18.09.59	26.10.59
23584	28.07.59	15.09.59						

CHAPTER EIGHT

METROPOLITAN RAILWAY COACHING STOCK

The Metropolitan Railway's coaching stock embraces a chapter which is totally separate from its saloon stock. Suffice to say that the great majority of it offered passenger accommodation in compartment form, with access being via outward-opening swing doors. The Metropolitan Railway always faced a dilemma when ordering new rolling stock, which was because of its 'main line' status, coupled with having to compete with the Great Central Railway, which not only ran parallel to it (north of Finchley Road to Harrow-on-the-Hill) but shared its tracks (Harrow-on-the-Hill to Aylesbury and beyond). Compartment stock usually won hands down on the outer suburban services, while inner suburban routes were the mainstay of the saloon type vehicles. Notwithstanding this, the Uxbridge line operated a mixture of both for many years.

THE RIGID EIGHT-WHEELERS

Five coaches built by the Oldbury Carriage & Wagon Co. in 1866 survived into LPTB ownership to operate on the Metropolitan's most rural branch line between Quainton Road and Brill. These comprised one first class coach, two third class brake coaches and two third class coaches, although one in service was more than adequate to meet the derisory traffic offering. They had all been rebuilt between 1902 and 1907. In addition, two other coaches survived into the LPTB era and were built in 1883–84 by Brown Marshalls.

Not surprisingly, the new LPTB decided that the Brill branch was uneconomic and set about closing it. The last trains ran on 30 November 1935, the seven coaches being scrapped early the following year.

No.	Type	Built	Builder	Rebuilt	Disposal
41	Brake 3rd	1866	Oldbury C&W Co.	1907	26.02.36
44	1st	1866	Oldbury C&W Co.	1902	26.02.36
45	Brake 3rd	1866	Oldbury C&W Co.	1907	26.02.36
72	3rd	1866	Oldbury C&W Co.	1903	26.02.36
89	3rd	1866	Oldbury C&W Co.	1903	26.02.36
232	3rd	1883	Brown-Marshall	–	26.02.36
295	3rd	1884	Brown-Marshall	–	26.02.36

Opposite page top Only two of the rigid eight-wheeler coaches of 1883–84 vintage remained when the LPTB took over the Metropolitan Railway's stock in 1933. In that year, No.295 is seen at Quainton Road. *H.C. Casserley*

Opposite page bottom The other five coaches kept for the sparse Brill branch service were of 1866 vintage and were rebuilt in 1902–07. No.41 is seen at Quainton Road in 1935 on a service to Brill, the year the line closed to the public. *Photomatic*

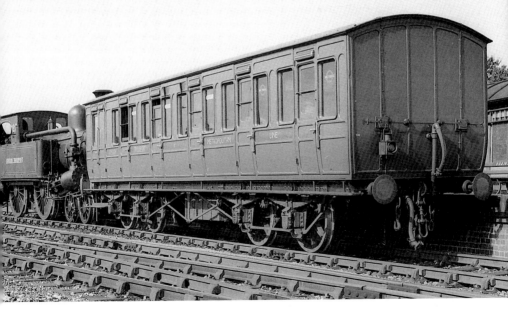

THE ASHBURY STOCK

The quality of the rolling stock providing the Metropolitan Railway's 'main line' services to Aylesbury, Verney Junction and Chesham was called into question in the late 1890s, which comprised both four-wheeled and rigid wheelbase vehicles, and as a result new locomotive-hauled carriages were ordered.

The first order, for four six-coach sets, was placed with the Ashbury Railway Carriage & Iron Co., and built in 1898. The coaches became known as the 'Ashbury' stock, even though other companies built subsequent batches. It was also known as 'Bogie' stock.

The vehicles were 42ft 4¾in long over buffers and 8ft 8in wide over the exterior grab rails, had elliptical roofs on which 'torpedo' ventilators were fixed. Brake coaches had a luggage compartment and five passenger compartments, while other coaches had seven compartments (second and third class) or six compartments (first class and composite cars), the latter type being arranged so that passengers had more leg room. Seating in all classes of compartment was ten, five on each side. This was the first Metropolitan Railway stock to be provided with electric lighting from new.

The success of these coaches resulted in a further five six-coach sets being ordered, the first being in service in 1900. Two sets were built by Ashbury, two by Cravens and one in the Metropolitan's workshops at Neasden – it was the original intention for them all to be built at Neasden but existing work commitments prevented this. The grand total of 'Ashbury' stock was thus 9x6-car sets, 54 cars, which were numbered in the series 361–414. In Metropolitan Railway coaching stock tradition, they were numbered in order onwards from the last in the previous series with no distinction between vehicle types. Each train set comprised six different vehicles and was numbered as follows:

Builder	Date	Brake 2nd	2nd	1st	Composite	3rd	Brake 3rd
Ashbury	1898	373	369	361	365	377	381
Ashbury	1898	374	370	362	366	378	382
Ashbury	1898	375	371	363	367	379	383
Ashbury	1898	376	372	364	368	380	384
Metropolitan Railway	1900	395	400	405	410	390	385
Cravens	1900	396	401	406	411	391	386
Cravens	1900	397	402	407	412	392	387
Ashbury	1900	398	403	408	413	393	388
Ashbury	1900	399	404	409	414	394	389

An Ashbury stock train is seen on the southbound at Willesden Green. Although withdrawn from service, most of these trains were stored during the Second World War. *Real Photographs Co.*

The fleet of 54 cars was subsequently augmented to 58. Two coaches were rebuilt at Neasden from two cars that were first built in 1899 by Brown Marshall's as part of a six-coach set for electrification trials on the Metropolitan District Railway between Earl's Court and High Street Kensington, which took place in 1899–1900. They became 415 (1st class) and 416 (2nd class) although the latter became a 3rd class car after the abolition of 2nd class in 1905–06.

The other two coaches, numbered 417 and 418, came from the Metropolitan Railway's own electrification experiments at Wembley Park, also in 1899–1900. They, too, had been stored after the experiments ceased and were believed to have been similar to the production 'Ashbury' stock of the same era.

In the meantime, the Metropolitan Railway had decided to convert two four-coach sets of Ashbury stock to electric working, each to be worked with a BW 150hp 'Saloon' stock motor car of the 1904–05 batches, at one end of the train. The cars so converted were:

3rd class DTs	384	387		
3rd class Trailers	372	380	392	402
1st class Trailers	364	407		

The driving trailers were converted from third class brake coaches. These had the narrow look-out windows at their outer ends replaced by a wide pair of windows, which were separated by a narrow vertical rib. Third class trailers 372 and 402 were originally second class. One of these trains was in service in late-1905, the other in early-1906. The intention was for them to be used as 'electric' trains to Harrow-on-the-Hill, from where the saloon motor car would be detached and be replaced by a steam locomotive for its onward journey. They would also be available for working on the Inner Circle in an emergency.

A more ambitious scheme was then implemented by the Metropolitan to form two eight-coach all-electric trains from the Ashbury fleet. The four motor coaches, converted from brake coaches, were each equipped with BTH 200hp motors. The number of passenger compartments were reduced in each by one, that removed being converted into a double-door luggage compartment and the former luggage area housing the electrical equipment. The converted cars were as follows:

3rd class DM	376	388	397	398	
3rd class Trailer	369	373	377	381	393	403
1st class Trailer	361	408			
Composite Trailer	365	368	412	413	

Initially, these two converted train sets operated in seven-car formations in 1906. Two third class vehicles (373 and 381) were not ready until 1907. This was because they had to be converted from brake coaches, requiring extensive reconstruction.

The first four-coach sets that were converted were by now regarded as 'semi-converted' and were in fact used very little, mainly because the trains were too heavy for the saloon stock BW 150hp motor cars. The answer was to form two six-coach trains for which four new motor cars were required. These were obtained by converting and adapting the two driving trailers (384 and 387) of the 1905/06 'semi-converted' trains and received BTH 200hp motors, and two coaches from the Wembley Park electrification experiments of 1899 (q.v. above). The latter pair were given the numbers 417 and 418 – at the end of the Ashbury stock number series. These were given spare BW 150hp equipment. The trains each included one third class trailer from the 1907 conversions – this because eight-coach sets were not required at the time, seven being sufficient for the traffic offering. The two six-coach trains comprised the following coaches:

3rd class DM	384*	387*	417§	418§		
3rd class Trailer	372†	373‡	380†	381‡	392†	402†
1st class Trailer	364†	407†				

* Former driving trailers.
† From 1905–06 'semi-converted' sets.
‡ From 1907 conversions.
§ Former experimental motor coaches of 1899.

The above coaches were converted by 1908, making a total of 26 'Ashbury' electric coaches. Of the remaining 32 steam-hauled coaches, one (No.362) was scrapped after a collision at Baker Street on 14 June 1925. The others were converted to electric working in 1921–24 for use with existing motor coaches of either the saloon or the compartment type. Six, however, were converted to driving trailers (378, 390, 394, 400, 401 and 404) and were given driving controls at one end with three separate cab windows.

In electric form, the Ashbury stock worked the Uxbridge line services from 11 July 1906, either as complete trains or with motor cars of other stocks. They also worked on the Stanmore line when it opened in 1932.

The London Passenger Transport Board therefore inherited 57 coaches of Ashbury stock of 1898–1900 vintage and renumbered them – see list opposite. Their replacement on the Uxbridge line by Metadyne P stock began in 1939, ordered under the 1935–40 New Works Programme. The outbreak of the Second World War deferred much of their scrapping because of the Government's requirement that withdrawn rolling stock should be retained for emergency use. In fact, one unserviceable car was previously written off in 1936, along with three others in 1940–41. One went to the Admiralty in Weymouth for wartime use in 1943 and another was written off in 1944.

Two three-coach sets were reconverted to steam operation for push-pull working on the Chesham shuttle service in 1940–41, with control equipment being fitted to the former driving trailer cars, where one such set is seen on the single line. *Photomatic*

Because the electrification of the Metropolitan Line north of Rickmansworth was deferred because of hostilities, it was decided to operate the Chalfont – Chesham shuttle service with dedicated three-car sets of Ashbury stock in push-pull mode with steam locomotives. The intention was to provide three such trains, because a passing loop on the single line branch was proposed, which would have required two trains in service and one spare. In the event, this loop was never built and two sets (one for service, one as a spare) were sufficient – the option for the third set was not taken up. Therefore, just two three-coach sets were re-converted to steam operation in 1940–41. These six coaches were renumbered at the end of the locomotive-hauled coaching stock series and also included provision for the third set.

The other 45 coaches were stored until after the war, 39 of them being outstabled in the sidings at Willesden Green (24 cars) and at the incomplete Ruislip depot (15 cars). After the war ended, they were scrapped in 1945–46.

DRIVING MOTOR COACHES – 8

Orig. No.	Date	Builder	LT No.	Push-Pull Conv.	Date	Disposal
384	1898	Ashbury	2760			27.06.45
387	1900	Cravens	2761	512	14.12.40	
417	1899	Met. Rly	2762			27.06.45
418	1899	Met. Rly	2763	513	12.10.40	
376	1898	Ashbury	2764			20.06.45
388	1900	Ashbury	2765			17.09.45
397	1900	Cravens	2766			20.06.45
398	1900	Ashbury	2767			17.09.45

DRIVING TRAILERS – 6

Orig. No.	Date	Builder	LT No.	Push-Pull Conv.	Date	Disposal
378	1898	Ashbury	6700			30.05.46
390	1900	Met. Rly.	6701			11.06.46
394	1900	Ashbury	6702	518	09.11.40	
400	1900	Met. Rly.	6703	519	14.12.40	
401	1900	Cravens	6704			30.05.46
404	1900	Ashbury	6705			11.06.46

FIRST CLASS TRAILERS – 16

Orig. No.	Date	Builder	LT No.	Push-Pull Conv.	Date	Disposal
361	1898	Ashbury	9700			06.06.45
364	1898	Ashbury	9701			27.06.45
368	1898	Ashbury	9702	515	19.10.40	
407	1900	Cravens	9703			20.06.45
408	1900	Cravens	9704			07.03.44
412	1900	Ashbury	9705	516	14.12.40	
363	1898	Ashbury	9706			17.09.45
366	1898	Ashbury	9707			26.07.40
367	1898	Ashbury	9708			30.05.46
405	1900	Met. Rly	9709			30.05.46
406	1900	Cravens	9710			11.06.46
409	1900	Ashbury	9711			02.01.46
410	1900	Met. Rly	9712			17.09.45
411	1900	Cravens	9713			06.06.45
414	1900	Ashbury	9714			11.06.46
415	1899	Brown Marshall	9715			02.01.46

THIRD CLASS TRAILERS – 27

Orig. No.	Date	Builder	LT No.	Disposal
365	1898	Ashbury	9746	21.06.41
413	1900	Ashbury	9747	26.02.36
369	1898	Ashbury	9748	17.09.45
372	1898	Ashbury	9749	17.09.45
373	1898	Ashbury	9750	06.06.45
377	1898	Ashbury	9751	17.09.45
380	1898	Ashbury	9752	27.06.45
381	1898	Ashbury	9753	27.06.45
392	1900	Cravens	9754	11.03.41
393	1900	Ashbury	9755	20.06.45
402	1900	Cravens	9756	17.09.45
403	1900	Ashbury	9757	20.06.45
370	1898	Ashbury	9758	17.07.43
371	1898	Ashbury	9759	02.07.46
379	1898	Ashbury	9760	02.07.46
391	1900	Cravens	9761	02.01.46
416	1899	Brown Marshall	9762	02.07.46
374	1898	Ashbury	9763	02.07.46
375	1898	Ashbury	9764	30.05.46
382	1898	Ashbury	9765	30.05.46
383	1898	Ashbury	9766	02.01.46
385	1900	Met. Rly	9767	02.07.46
386	1900	Cravens	9768	11.06.46
389	1900	Ashbury	9769	06.06.45
395	1900	Met. Rly	9770	02.01.46
396	1900	Cravens	9771	06.06.45
399	1900	Ashbury	9772	11.06.46

Seven-compartment brake coach 485, built in 1920, seen in March 1934, still in Metropolitan Railway varnished condition and with panelled lining. A feature of the Metropolitan's main line aspirations is the destination board in the middle of the train above the windows. Note the shoebeams found on brake coaches, which were added to reduce arcing over current rail gaps from 1916. *LT Museum*

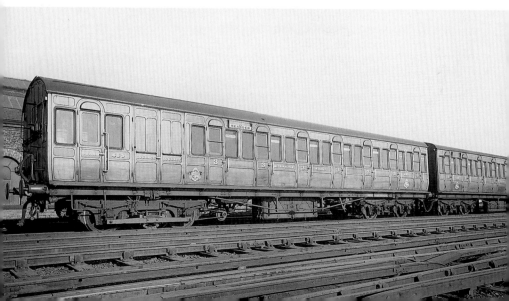

THE 'DREADNOUGHT' STOCK

In an attempt to raise standards in rolling stock provision and comfort, to equal that already provided by the Great Central Railway, the Metropolitan took ten of its 1905 1st class saloon stock driving trailers, made spare as a result of previously reducing Circle Line trains from five to four cars, and had them converted into what were the forerunners of the famous 'Dreadnought' coaches for 'main line' services. The ten vehicles were converted by the Metropolitan Amalgamated Railway Carriage & Wagon Company to form two five-coach sets, and were as follows:

CT No.	New No.	Converted to	CT No.	New No.	Converted to
38	419	7-compartment 1st	48	424	9-compartment 3rd
34	420	7-compartment 1st	22	425	7 compartment 3rd + Brake
45	421	7-compartment 1st	41	426	7 compartment 3rd + Brake
44	422	7-compartment 1st	42	427	7 compartment 3rd + Brake
30	423	9-compartment 3rd	26	428	7 compartment 3rd + Brake

It will be seen that there were three types of vehicle constructed – Brake 3rd (7 compartments), 3rd class (9 compartments) and 1st class (7 compartments). Each of the two five-car trains comprised two brake 3rds and two 1st class cars, plus one 3rd class coach. It had been the practice for the Metropolitan to number cars from '1' upwards for each type of car (hence, for the Saloon stock, there was a 'No.1' motor, trailer and control trailer) but the main line locomotive-hauled coaches were numbered onwards from where the previous builds had left off. In this case, the last number was 418, which belonged to the 'Ashbury' stock of 1898–1900. The 'Dreadnought' coaches were thus numbered from 419 upwards and no distinction was made in numbering between the different types of vehicle.

The success of the 1910 conversions led to the construction of three more batches of Dreadnought stock, all built by the Metropolitan Amalgamated R.C. & W.Co. The first, in 1912 and comprising four five-car trains, followed on close behind the experimental conversions. These were:

Numbers	Type
429–436	7 compartment 1st
437–440	9 compartment 3rd
441–448	7 compartment 3rd + Brake

The seven-compartment first-class coaches were much roomier than their third-class counterparts. Coach 431 of 1912 vintage stands at Aylesbury on 2 May 1936. First-class accommodation on the Underground had just a little over five years to operate before it was finally abolished. *H.C. Casserley*

Initially, the trains were fitted with gas lighting of the Pintsch type but by 1918 they (along with other remaining gas-lit coaches) had been converted to electric lighting. The trains, when hauled by electric locomotives, had rather a leisurely acceleration, which did little for the Metropolitan's time keeping in the central area. This was because the short span between the shoes of the locomotives was insufficient to bridge the current rail gaps at points and crossovers, over which locomotives had to coast – it was undesirable even to try to accelerate over current rail gaps! To overcome the problem, the brake coaches of one train were fitted with collector shoes and shoebeams on the outer end bogies and these were connected through to the locomotive by a bus-line cable at solebar level. In 1916, all such train sets were fitted with shoebeams and shoes, not only to improve the acceleration rate in the central area, but to prevent arcing over current rail gaps which then infringed the 'blackout' regulations during the First World War.

More Dreadnought coaches were built in 1920, with a final batch in 1923 (ordered in 1919 and 1922 respectively), all of which had electric lighting from new. The 1920 order comprised 42 coaches to make up 'seven six-car trains', although the actual types of vehicles provided did not match up with the previous formations. Four new steam locomotives were also obtained at about the same time (1920–21) and there were also timetable improvements to the main line services from 1 January 1922.

The 1923 batch of new coaches was required 'for the Watford extension' and that order comprised 20 cars formed into three six-car rakes, with two coaches spare. The cars and types can be summarised as follows:

Year	Numbers	Type
1920	449–462	7-compartment 1st
1920	463–482	9-compartment 3rd
1920	483–490	7 compartment 3rd + Brake
1923	491–496	6-compartment 3rd + Brake
1923	497–504	9-compartment 3rd
1923	505–507	7-compartment 1st
1923	508–510	7 compartment 1st/3rd

There were thus 92 coaches at maximum, of the following types:

	1910	1912	1920	1923	Total
Brake 3rd 7-compartment	4	8	8	–	20
Brake 3rd 6-compartment	–	–	–	6	6
3rd class 9-compartment	2	4	20	8	34
1st class 7-compartment	4	8	14	3	29
1st & 3rd 7-compartment	–	–	–	3	3
Total:	**10**	**20**	**42**	**20**	**92**

Whilst the Dreadnought coaches were of a standard equivalent to the stock used on the neighbouring Great Central Railway, there remained a problem with interior heating. The electric locomotives were unable to provide 'steam' heating and thus travel between the City, Baker Street and Rickmansworth was without heating, as were coaches that were stabled between the peak service. What turned out to be inadequate electrical heaters were installed in 1921, only to be replaced from 1926 by heaters in greater number. The supply for the lighting was from a dynamo and battery, even when the train was travelling on the electric system – the collector shoes were provided for heating and to bridge rail gaps.

When new, the interior layout was arranged in semi-open form in groups of two or three compartments, with each group of compartments linked by a central corridor. The third class nine-compartment coaches were arranged 3+3+3 while the first class and brake coaches were arranged 2+3+2. However, it was decided to increase seating capacity wherever possible and from 1930 all coaches were re-arranged in single compartment form, each having a pair of longitudinal facing seats. The compartment next to the guard on the brake coaches was designated as 'Ladies Only'.

The 1923 maximum of 92 Dreadnought coaches did not last for long in their own right (although all but two survived in some form). In 1929 a total of 15 Dreadnought coaches were converted to EMU working, to run with six new 'MV' motor coaches, making three seven-car trains. Although no longer intended to be locomotive-hauled on a regular basis, the coaches retained their own numbers after conversion because they could, if need be, still be used in locomotive-hauled train formations – it was not until the LPTB took over the Metropolitan Railway in 1933 that these coaches acquired 'EMU' series numbers. The 15 conversions comprised six 7-compartment 1st class trailers, three 9-compartment 3rd class trailers and six 8-compartment 3rd class control trailers.

The Dreadnought cars involved were as follows:

No.	Year	Steam Stock Type	Conversion To	EMU No.
460	1920	1st class 7-compartment	1st class 7-compartment trailer	9716
461	1920	1st class 7-compartment	1st class 7-compartment trailer	9717
462	1920	1st class 7-compartment	1st class 7-compartment trailer	9718
476	1920	3rd class 9-compartment	3rd class 9-compartment trailer	9773
477	1920	3rd class 9-compartment	3rd class 8-compartment control trailer	6706
478	1920	3rd class 9-compartment	3rd class 8-compartment control trailer	6707
479	1920	3rd class 9-compartment	3rd class 8-compartment control trailer	6708
480	1920	3rd class 9-compartment	3rd class 8-compartment control trailer	6709
481	1920	3rd class 9-compartment	3rd class 8-compartment control trailer	6710
482	1920	3rd class 9-compartment	3rd class 8-compartment control trailer	6711
500	1923	3rd class 9-compartment	3rd class 9-compartment trailer	9774
501	1923	3rd class 9-compartment	3rd class 9-compartment trailer	9775
505	1923	1st class 7-compartment	1st class 7-compartment trailer	9719
506	1923	1st class 7-compartment	1st class 7-compartment trailer	9720
507	1923	1st class 7-compartment	1st class 7-compartment trailer	9721

After the conversions, therefore, the locomotive-hauled Dreadnought stock comprised 77 coaches, which is the total that the LPTB inherited in 1933.

	1910	1912	1920	1923	Total
Brake 3rd 7-compartment	4	8	8	–	20
Brake 3rd 6-compartment	–	–	–	6	6
3rd class 9-compartment	2	4	13	6	25
1st class 7-compartment	4	8	11	–	23
1st & 3rd 7-compartment	–	–	–	3	3

Three further cars were converted in 1935 to lengthen the three seven-car MV stock EMU trains to eight cars and at the same time converting them to 'MW' stock. The three cars were as follows:

No.	Year	Steam Stock Type	Conversion To	EMU No.
497	1923	3rd class 9-compartment	3rd class 9-compartment trailer	9800
498	1923	3rd class 9-compartment	3rd class 9-compartment trailer	9801
499	1923	3rd class 9-compartment	3rd class 9-compartment trailer	9802

The Dreadnought stock then comprised 74 cars, as under:

	1910	1912	1920	1923	Total
Brake 3rd 7-compartment	4	8	8	–	20
Brake 3rd 6-compartment	–	–	–	6	6
3rd class 9-compartment	2	4	13	3	22
1st class 7-compartment	4	8	11	–	23
1st & 3rd 7-compartment	–	–	–	3	3

In the 1930s, experimentation with exterior liveries took place. One train set (comprising coaches 419, 429, 437, 465, 488 and 493) was painted olive green with a red waist, while another (coaches 434, 441, 457, 466, 486 and 504) was painted light green with a red waist. Neither were satisfactory and the experiment was not pursued. In the late-1930s, the Dreadnought coach fleet was fitted with ex-District type K2 bogies to try and improve on poor ride quality.

Under part of the 1935–40 New Works Programme, it was planned to absorb most of the Dreadnought coaches into what became the T EMU stock for the proposed electrification of the Metropolitan Line from Rickmansworth to Amersham and Chesham. The fleet then comprised 74 coaches and it was intended to scrap all ten 1910 conversions, plus 1912 3rd class brake coach No.447 that was damaged at Rickmansworth on 15 September 1939, making a total of 63 cars to be so treated. To that end, the conversions commenced in 1940. However, the Second World War put most of the 1935–30 New Works Programme into abeyance and only seven Dreadnought coaches were actually converted at Acton Works to run as T stock. They were:

No.	Year	Steam Stock Type	Conversion To	EMU No.
484	1920	3rd class 9-compartment	3rd class 8-compartment control trailer	6743
487	1920	3rd class 9-compartment	3rd class 8-compartment control trailer	6746
449	1920	1st class 7-compartment	1st class 7-compartment trailer	9812
455	1920	1st class 7-compartment	1st class 7-compartment trailer	9818
457	1920	1st class 7-compartment	1st class 7-compartment trailer	9820
458	1920	1st class 7-compartment	1st class 7-compartment trailer	9821
504	1923	3rd class 9-compartment	3rd class 9-compartment trailer	9842

Apart from coach 447 (q.v. above) and 1910 car No.424, both of which were scrapped on 6 December 1939, all other Dreadnought coaches were to remain available for service, being hauled by locomotives – electric from the City and Baker Street to Rickmansworth and steam beyond. The net balance from the pre-1939 figure of 74 was a reduction of nine cars, two being scrapped and seven being converted to T stock, making 65 in all and summarised as follows:

	1910	1912	1920	1923	Total
Brake 3rd 7-compartment	4	7	6	–	17
Brake 3rd 6-compartment	–	–	–	6	6
3rd class 9-compartment	1	4	13	2	20
1st class 7-compartment	4	8	7	–	19
1st & 3rd 7-compartment	–	–	–	3	3

The Dreadnought coaches converted into EMU working had their side buffers removed but remained different from their true EMU counterparts in having the centre buffing between cars in wood, whereas true T stock had metal buffing gear.

First class accommodation on the Underground was an early casualty of the wartime situation. The facilities were withdrawn on the Aylesbury and Watford lines on 6 October 1941, although other 'surface' lines had succumbed previously on 1 February 1940 (the Hammersmith & City had lost its first class on 4 May 1936). With all coaches being one class only, the seven-compartment (non-brake) coaches always remained roomier and for a time retained the armrests, but these were soon sewn up until the seats were changed at a later date. The former 3rd class cars always had plain panelled ceilings, whereas the former first class coaches retained the decorative ceilings.

The Dreadnought coaches worked on the Metropolitan's 'main line' services which, until 1936, included workings beyond Aylesbury to Verney Junction, and between 1943 and 1948 beyond Aylesbury to Quainton Road, albeit infrequently. The coaches also worked on the Chesham shuttle service until 1940, when specially converted 'Ashbury' stock took over, operating as 'push-pull' trains (q.v. above). Red-painted outer ends were applied to the brake coaches from the early-1950s.

THIRD CLASS BRAKE COACHES (7-COMPARTMENT) – 20

No.	Built	No.	Built	EMU Conv.	Date	Disposal
425	1910*	447	1912			06.12.39
426	1910*	448	1912			
427	1910*	483	1920			
428	1910*	484	1920	6743	27.07.40	
441	1912	485	1920			
442	1912	486	1920			
443	1912	487	1920	6746	29.06.40	
444	1912	488	1920			
445	1912	489	1920			
446	1912	490	1920			

* Converted from 'Saloon' driving trailers built 1905.

THIRD CLASS BRAKE COACHES (6-COMPARTMENT) – 6

No.	Built	No.	Built
491	1923	494	1923
492	1923	495	1923
493	1923	496	1923

THIRD CLASS COACHES (9-COMPARTMENT) – 22

No.	Built	Disposal	No.	Built	EMU Conv.	Date
423	1910*		468	1920		
424	1910*	06.12.39	469	1920		
437	1912		470	1920		
438	1912		471	1920		
439	1912		472	1920		
440	1912		473	1920		
463	1920		474	1920		
464	1920		475	1920		
465	1920		497	1923	9800	22.06.35
466	1920		498	1923	9801	08.10.35
467	1920		499	1923	9802	22.06.35

* Converted from 'Saloon' driving trailers built 1905

FIRST CLASS COACHES (7-COMPARTMENT) – 23

No.	Built	No.	Built	EMU Conv.	Date
419	1910*	449	1920	9812	03.08.40
420	1910*	450	1920		
421	1910	451	1920		
422	1910	452	1920		
429	1912	453	1920		
430	1912	454	1920		
431	1912	455	1920	9818	06.07.40
432	1912	456	1920		
433	1912	457	1920	9820	29.06.40
434	1912	458	1920	9821	08.06.40
435	1912	459	1920		
436	1912				

* Converted from 'Saloon' driving trailers built 1905

COMPOSITE FIRST/THIRD CLASS COACHES (7-COMPARTMENT) – 3

No.	Built	No.	Built	No.	Built
508	1923	509	1923	510	1923

The Metropolitan operated two Pullman cars on its longer-distance services to Aylesbury and Chesham, but these had to succumb to a red livery in the early-1920s, because of the tunnel conditions. One of the two coaches is formed in a train at Neasden on 1 November 1933. Metropolitan Railway locomotive No.10 is still in Metropolitan Railway condition. *LT Museum*

METROPOLITAN PULLMAN COACHES

A facility unique to Underground operations was the provision of a refreshment service, using two Pullman cars, which were ordered by the Metropolitan Railway for its 'main line' services. This was seen as direct competition with the neighbouring Great Central Railway, who the Metropolitan saw as a direct threat in poaching their first class passengers. To that end, two Pullman cars were built by Birmingham for the Pullman Car Company but were fitted out to the Metropolitan's specifications. The cars were named 'Galatea' and 'Mayflower'. Passenger services with them on Mondays to Saturdays began on 1 June 1910 and until the Dreadnought coaches became available at a later date, they initially worked in Ashbury stock formations, with one Pullman car per train. Because end gangways were never fitted to the coaching stock with which they worked, the end doors on the Pullman cars were never used, passenger access being via inward-opening hinged single doors at the car ends.

Each Pullman car had seating for 19 passengers in individually upholstered armchairs, and each car had a pantry and toilet. The interior of each car differed. One had a mahogany finish and green upholstery while the other had an oak finish with crimson upholstery. Each table was provided with the traditional Pullman style ornate table lamp. The exteriors of each car comprised six large windows with an oval (frosted) window at each end, and were finished in umber below the waist and cream above, with gold lining.

The tunnel working conditions of the Metropolitan did nothing to keep their exterior finish smart, and in the early-1920s the external livery was changed to all-over crimson when the cars were overhauled.

The service came to an end on 7 October 1939, shortly after the outbreak of the Second World War – such facilities were deemed inappropriate under the circumstances, although first class accommodation on coaching stock continued on the Watford and Aylesbury services until 6 October 1941. The two Pullman coaches were disposed of by early-1941, putting an end to any intended resumption of such services after the war.

However, the idea of a 'refreshment' service was revived in May 1951, and perhaps not surprisingly, only the Metropolitan's Aylesbury line was deemed suitable for such a service. It was considered by some that a 'buffet' car service on the Metropolitan Line would take up valuable passenger accommodation, and although there were no operating or engineering objections to the scheme in principle, there was little support for the idea from higher management (some of whom who were against it described the idea as no more than 'a stunt') and by the end of 1951, the scheme was formally laid to rest.

THE ROTHSCHILD SALOON

Another luxurious carriage that the Metropolitan Railway owned was the 'Rothschild Saloon', although it started life as two individual six-wheeled coaches. The original pair were built by Brown Marshall's in 1895 and the Metropolitan provided them for the millionaire Ferdinand de Rothschild, whose country seat was at Halton, near Wendover. The coaches were formed into specific trains to operate to and from Baker Street to Rothschild's requirements and this arrangement continued for several years.

In 1905, however, it had been decided to make one longer coach out of the two, which was done by splicing the bodies together, thus creating two saloons in one vehicle. The reconstructed coach was provided with bogies and electric lighting replaced the original gas lighting. Moveable chairs and tables were provided in each saloon, instead of fixed settees as hitherto. The rebuilt coach was completed in early-1907.

Whilst its use in later years was restricted, it did from 1912 substitute from time to time for a Pullman car if required for maintenance or overhaul. The vehicle passed into LPTB ownership on 1 July 1933 and what is believed to have been its last official use was an inspection of the Brill branch on 23 July 1935, prior to the line's closure on 30 November 1935. It had passed into the London Transport 'service stock' fleet in May 1935 and was then declared 'withdrawn' but was kept in Neasden depot for another ten years until written off on 30 May 1946. London Transport allocated the stock number S900 to it.

The Rothschild Saloon coach seen in a sorry state in Neasden depot, prior to scrapping in 1946. Its last recorded use was in an inspection train on the Brill branch in 1935 just prior to closure. It originally comprised two separate shorter vehicles and was converted to this form in 1907. *Charles F. Klapper/LURS*

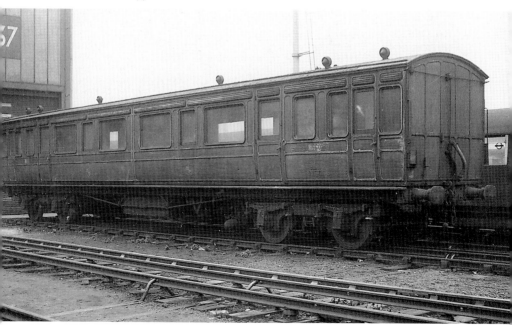

THE METROPOLITAN SHUTTLE COACHES

Mention has already been made of two 'Saloon' stock motor cars that were badly damaged as a result of serious incidents. The first involved 1905-built motor coach 46 in a collision in fog at West Hampstead on 26 October 1907, the second on 6 October 1908 when 1906-built motor car 69 was badly damaged by fire at Swiss Cottage. The remains of the former were adapted in 1909 to serve as a gauging car prior to the introduction of the Pullman carriages in 1910. After this work had been completed, both cars remained stored at Neasden while decisions were made on their future.

The MCW&F Co. were awarded a contract to rebuild the two cars into double-ended motor cars of the compartment type for the Metropolitan's shuttle services, which was undertaken in 1910. Each car had an elliptical roof and a cab at each end, and one end of each had a luggage compartment behind the cab. Between this and the other cab were six passenger compartments, the two centre ones being for first class passengers. Although intended to operate as single cars, couplings were provided on each to enable a saloon stock driving trailer to be added if necessary. Motor car No.46 retained its BW 150hp equipment, while No.69 was fitted with similar equipment in place of its BTH 200hp equipment, the latter considered as rather wasteful on a single car.

The cars were initially used on the Uxbridge line shuttle services (the development of Metroland was still awaited – the line ran through almost all open countryside, even though additional stations had been provided at Rayners Lane, Eastcote and Ickenham soon after the line's opening) but in 1918 were transferred to operate between Edgware Road and Kensington (Addison Road). For this service, the cab doors had to be modified. Instead of opening outwards like the passenger doors, they were changed to open inwards – the previous arrangement was undesirable in tunnel sections – this was done in early-1921. After the Watford branch opened in 1925 they were transferred to operate the Rickmansworth – Watford shuttle service. When the LPTB inherited the Metropolitan Railway in 1933 the Rickmansworth – Watford shuttle was an early casualty, the service being withdrawn on 21 January 1934. Thereafter, the cars operated on the Stanmore – Wembley Park shuttles and were renumbered 2768 (ex–46) and 2769 (ex–69) with their new owners. These two numbers continued at the end of the Ashbury stock motor car series.

The less reliable car of the pair, 2768, was withdrawn in early-1938 and scrapped, but 2769 remained in service on the Stanmore branch until it became part of the Bakerloo Line in November 1939, latterly having a saloon stock driving trailer added as a permanent feature. The car was initially stored after withdrawal and, along with a number of Saloon stock cars, was converted to become a tank target unit at Acton in September 1942, from when it was written off LT's record books.

Orig. No.	LT No.	Disposal
46	**2768**	22.02.38
69	**2769**	01.09.42

CHAPTER NINE

METROPOLITAN RAILWAY MULTIPLE UNIT COMPARTMENT STOCK

The mainstay of the Watford – Baker Street/City services of the Metropolitan Line was what became the T stock, although occasional trips by this stock to the Uxbridge branch were not unheard of. It was the growth of traffic in the north-west suburbs and the opening of the Watford extension in 1925 that led to the stock being built, although the first coaches were replacement for saloon motor cars.

The cgT stock built new at its maximum comprised 60 driving motor cars, 24 control trailers (the Metropolitan preferred to call them DRIVING trailers) and 48 trailers. All was not so simple and straightforward, however, as there were four distinct builds and to these were added at various times a further eight control trailers and 17 trailers, converted from locomotive-hauled Dreadnought coaches.

After a trial with two saloon type motor coaches with Metropolitan-Vickers equipment built in 1925 it was decided to purchase 12 motor coaches with compartment type bodies using Metropolitan Vickers electrical equipment. The first six cars (numbered 200–205) had no side buffers but were fitted with buckeye couplers and had Westinghouse air brakes. These six cars were provided as replacements for six saloon stock motor cars that ran with Ashbury (or 'Bogie') stock trailers of 1898–1900 vintage, although it was possible for saloon stock motors to be substituted if a new stock car was out of service for maintenance purposes. Three eight-car W stock trains were thus formed. The other six new motor cars (206–211) had side buffers, screw couplings and vacuum brakes. Although similar to cars 200–205 they were 1ft 8ins longer, at 55ft 5ins overall. To run with these cars, 15 steam stock 'Dreadnought' coaches were suitably converted, comprising six 1st class trailers, six 3rd class control trailers and three 3rd class trailers. It was thus possible to form three seven-car trains of MV stock, although the converted trailers could revert to locomotive-hauled operation if need be.

All 12 new 1927 motor cars had Metropolitan-Vickers electrical equipment and had five passenger compartments for 50 seated passengers (ten per compartment, five a side).

A further order for new stock was placed in 1929 with the Birmingham R.C. & W. Co. and comprised 30 motor cars, ten 3rd class control trailers, ten 1st class trailers and five 3rd class trailers. This batch of (1930) fulfilled four purposes:

- It enabled 5x7-car MW stock trains to be formed using ten motor coaches and all 25 of the new trailers/control trailers. The ten motor cars used here were interchangeable with 200–205 already in service.

- 2x8-car W stock trains were formed with four new motor cars and existing Ashbury trailers.

- A total of 12 new motors enabled 5x8 and 1x7-car VT stock trains to be formed, using saloon stock trailers.

- Four new motor coaches available as spares.

Seen approaching Rayners Lane, probably in about 1935, is a four-coach train comprising an MW stock motor and saloon trailers, with a saloon control trailer bringing up the rear. This type of train formation was designated VT stock. *Author's collection*

MW stock motors that operated with Ashbury trailers were designated W stock and one eight-coach formation is seen at Neasden. *Author's collection*

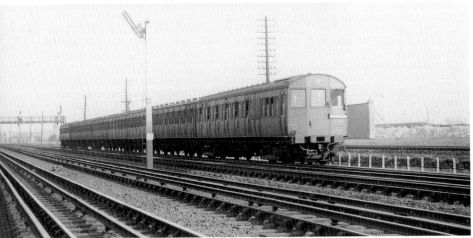

The six MV motor coaches were identifiable from others in having an extra beading line midway between the bottom of the windows and the buffers. One such coach is seen at Rickmansworth. *Photomatic*

The final batch of stock was also built by Birmingham and was delivered in 1932, comprising 65 vehicles – 18 motors, 14 3rd class control trailers, 14 1st class trailers and 19 3rd class trailers. This build of stock had steel body panels and gave a flush-sided finish to the cars. It was built to serve three purposes:

• More MW stock was formed – 7x8 cars used 14 vehicles from each type.

• The five extra 3rd class trailers were used to lengthen the 5x7-car MW stock trains of 1930 into eight-car formation. The five new trailers, although having steel body panels, were given mouldings, to match the slightly older cars. In retrospect, this seems a strange decision, bearing in mind the hotch-potch of vehicles in a standard Metropolitan train. For example, the VT and W stock mixtures and the usual variety of clerestory and elliptical roofs that would be found in saloon stock trains.

• The four additional motor cars were used to make up 2x7-car trains of VT stock (which utilised saloon stock trailers). The saloon stock motor cars replaced in the VT trains were converted to trailers.

The 1932 stock motor cars had GEC equipment and were designed to operate in multiple with the earlier MV-equipped cars. In the event, the two types were incompatible because of the difference in motor gearing and this reduced operating flexibility somewhat. The stock at this time thus comprised:

| | | New Stock | | | | Dreadnought Conversions | | |
		DM	CT	1T	3T	CT	1T	3T
5x8	'W' Stock	10	–	–	–	–	–	–
3x7	'MV' Stock	6	–	–	–	6	6	3
12x8	'MW' Stock	24	24	24	24	–	–	–
5x8	'VT' Stock	10	–	–	–	–	–	–
3x7	'VT' Stock	6	–	–	–	–	–	–
	Spare	4	–	–	–	–	–	–
Total:		60	24	24	24	6	6	3
Total Cars:			***132***				***15***	

In 1935 the three seven-car trains of MV stock were converted to have Westinghouse brakes and each were increased to eight cars by the conversion of three more Dreadnought coaches into 3rd class trailers, making 3x8 MW stock. The stock situation then was that there were 15x8 trains of MW stock (which utilised 30 motor coaches and all 90 trailers – 72 'new' and 18 conversions), while the other 30 motor coaches were used variously in W and VT stock trains (using Ashbury and Saloon stock trailers respectively) and for spares. The stock 'grand total' had thus risen to 150 cars – 132 'new' and 18 Dreadnought conversions. From 1935, the five-compartment motor coaches were converted into six-compartment 60-seat coaches by utilising the guard's compartment. This extra 10-seat compartment was reserved for, and designated, as 'Ladies Only'.

Part of the 1935–40 New Works programme proposed electrifying the Metropolitan Line from Rickmansworth to Amersham and Chesham, and envisaged the utilisation of all 60 motor coaches, the existing new and converted trailers, and the conversion of most of the remaining Dreadnought coaches to EMU working, with all trains being fitted with electro-pneumatic brakes and mercury retardation control. In the event, only one train (plus one odd car) was so equipped, which comprised two motor coaches, five ex-Dreadnought trailers and two ex-Dreadnought trailers (which became control trailers). All the stock involved, along with their original numbers, is summarised as follows:

ELECTRIC COMPARTMENT STOCK – BUILT NEW

Year	Nos	Type		Cars	Total	Stock	LT No.
1927	200–205	3rd Class DM	5-Compartments	6		W	2700–2705
1927	206–211	3rd Class DM	5-Compartments	6	12	MV	2706–2711
1930	212–241	3rd Class DM	5-Compartments	30		MW/W/VT	2712–2741
1930	511–520	1st Class Trailer	7-Compartments	10		MW	9722–9731
1930	521–525	3rd Class Trailer	9-Compartments	5		MW	9776–9780
1930	526–535	3rd Class DT	8-Compartments	10	55	MW	6712–6721
1932	242–259	3rd Class DM	5-Compartments	18		MW/VT	2742–2759
1932	536–549	3rd Class DT	8-Compartments	14		MW	6732–6735
1932	550–568	3rd Class Trailer	9-Compartments	19		MW	9781–9799
1932	569–582	1st Class Trailer	7-Compartments	14	65	MW	9732–9745

Total EMU Compartment Stock: 132

CONVERSIONS FROM 'DREADNOUGHT' STEAM STOCK

No.	Steam Stock Type		EMU Conversion		LT No.
(a) 15 Conversions in 1929:					
460	1st Class	7-Cpts	1st Class	7-Compartment Trailer	9716
461	1st Class	7-Cpts	1st Class	7-Compartment Trailer	9717
462	1st Class	7-Cpts	1st Class	7-Compartment Trailer	9718
476	3rd Class	9-Cpts	3rd Class	9-Compartment Trailer	9773
477	3rd Class	9-Cpts	3rd Class	8-Compartment Control Trailer	6706
478	3rd Class	9-Cpts	3rd Class	8-Compartment Control Trailer	6707
479	3rd Class	9-Cpts	3rd Class	8-Compartment Control Trailer	6708
480	3rd Class	9-Cpts	3rd Class	8-Compartment Control Trailer	6709
481	3rd Class	9-Cpts	3rd Class	8-Compartment Control Trailer	6710
482	3rd Class	9-Cpts	3rd Class	8-Compartment Control Trailer	6711
500	3rd Class	9-Cpts	3rd Class	9-Compartment Trailer	9774
501	3rd Class	9-Cpts	3rd Class	9-Compartment Trailer	9775
505	1st Class	7-Cpts	1st Class	7-Compartment Trailer	9719
506	1st Class	7-Cpts	1st Class	7-Compartment Trailer	9720
507	1st Class	7-Cpts	1st Class	7-Compartment Trailer	9721
(b) 3 Conversions in 1935:					
497	3rd Class	9-Cpts	3rd Class	9-Compartment Trailer	9800
498	3rd Class	9-Cpts	3rd Class	9-Compartment Trailer	9801
499	3rd Class	9-Cpts	3rd Class	9-Compartment Trailer	9802
(c) 7 Conversions in 1940:					
484	3rd Class	9-Cpts	3rd Class	8-Compartment Control Trailer	6743
487	3rd Class	9-Cpts	3rd Class	8-Compartment Control Trailer	6746
449	1st Class	7-Cpts	1st Class	7-Compartment Trailer	9812
455	1st Class	7-Cpts	1st Class	7-Compartment Trailer	9818
457	1st Class	7-Cpts	1st Class	7-Compartment Trailer	9820
458	1st Class	7-Cpts	1st Class	7-Compartment Trailer	9821
504	3rd Class	9-Cpts	3rd Class	9-Compartment Trailer	9842

From the 74 Dreadnought cars remaining before the beginning of the Second World War, 63 were to be converted to EMU working, while 11 were to be withdrawn and scrapped. The latter group comprised the ten 1910 conversions from 1905 saloon stock control trailers, plus one (No.447) which had been damaged and was considered to be beyond economical repair. The 63 scheduled to be converted to trailers and control trailers would have been numbered as detailed opposite (and indeed, q.v. above, seven already had been, but work stopped because of the war and subsequent postponement of the 1935–40 New Works Programme). Those seven that were actually converted and renumbered are shown opposite in bold.

A train of T stock, as the MV and MW stocks had collectively become, approaches Moorgate. *Photomatic*

3rd Class 7-Compartment Brakes to 3rd Class 8-Compartment Control Trailers:

1912	441	(6756)	1912	446	(6739)	1920	486	(6745)
1912	442	(6740)	1912	448	(6741)	1920	487	**6746**
1912	443	(6736)	1920	483	(6742)	1920	488	(6747)
1912	444	(6737)	1920	484	**6743**	1920	489	(6748)
1912	445	(6738)	1920	485	(6744)	1920	490	(6749)

3rd Class 6-Compartment Brakes to 3rd Class 8-Compartment Control Trailers:

1923	491	(6750)	1923	493	(6752)	1923	495	(6754)
1923	492	(6751)	1923	494	(6753)	1923	496	(6755)

1st/3rd 7-Compartment Brake to 1st Class 7-Compartment Trailer:

1923	508	(9803)

1st/3rd 7-Compartment Brake to 3rd Class 9-Compartment Trailers:

1923	509	(9843)	1923	510	(9844)

3rd Class 9-Compartment to 3rd Class 9-Compartment Trailers:

1912	437	(9823)	1920	466	(9830)	1920	473	(9837)
1912	438	(9824)	1920	467	(9831)	1920	474	(9838)
1912	439	(9825)	1920	468	(9832)	1920	475	(9839)
1912	440	(9826)	1920	469	(9833)	1923	502	(9840)
1920	463	(9827)	1920	470	(9834)	1923	503	(9841)
1920	464	(9828)	1920	471	(9835)	1923	504	**9842**
1920	465	(9829)	1920	472	(9836)			

1st Class 7-Compartment to 1st Class 7-Compartment Trailers:

1912	429	(9804)	1912	436	(9811)	1920	455	**9818**
1912	430	(9805)	1920	449	**9812**	1920	456	(9819)
1912	431	(9806)	1920	450	(9813)	1920	457	**9820**
1912	432	(9807)	1920	451	(9814)	1920	458	**9821**
1912	433	(9808)	1920	452	(9815)	1920	459	(9822)
1912	434	(9809)	1920	453	(9816)			
1912	435	(9810)	1920	454	(9817)			

Two of the coaches converted to EMU working (457 and 504) were previously in the experimental livery of bright green with red waists. The coaches converted to EMU working had their side buffers removed but remained different from their true EMU counterparts in having the centre buffing between cars in wood, whereas the T stock had metal buffer gear.

The decision to postpone the electrification to Amersham in April 1940 saw a directive issued to cover the situation to date. The stock comprised 58 MW-type motor cars (2707 and 2752 had already been withdrawn by this time), 30 control trailers and 90 trailers. It was proposed that five steam stock cars would be converted to control trailers (483, 484, 485, 487 and 490 to 6742, 6743, 6744, 6746 and 6749 respectively), five more to first class trailers (455–459 to 9818–9822) and five to 3rd class trailers (449, 508, 509, 510 and 505 to 9812, 9803, 9843, 9844 and 9842 respectively). This would then give 58 MW-type motors, 35 control trailers and 70 trailers for 16 trains (utilising 32 motors, 32 control trailers and 64 trailers), leaving 26 motors, three control trailers and six trailers spare. Even this plan, however, was not completed. There would be 5x6 and 3x7 rakes of Dreadnought stock left for the Aylesbury line service, leaving only 1x6 set spare. The correspondence on this subject quotes, "... traffic spare to be provided by a train hired from the LNER ...".

The last of this type to be built were the all-steel coaches built by Birmingham in 1933. In lined Metropolitan Railway livery, DM 254 (which was soon to become 2754) approaches Willesden Green. *Photomatic*

In the event, the T stock fleet comprised just 157 cars and the build-up of these from new and from conversions can be summarised as follows:

	What Became 'T' Stock				Former Loco. Conv'n				Trains	Notes
	DM	CT	1T	3T	CT	1T	3T			
1. 1927–29	6	–	–	–	–	–	–		3x8	W stock (200–205) using Ashbury trailers but with the facility to replace motors for maintenance purposes.
2. 1927–29	6	–	–	–	6	6	3		3x7	MV stock motors (206–211) using converted steam stock trailers, but with facility for trailers to revert to steam operation if required.
3. 1930	10	10	10	5	–	–	–	(a)	5x7	MW stock, with the 10 motor cars interchangeable with 200–205, and all trailers utilised.
	4	–	–	–	–	–	–	(b)	2x8	W stock using Ashbury trailers.
	12	–	–	–	–	–	–	(c)	5x8 1x7	VT stock using Saloon trailers.
	4	–	–	–	–	–	–	(d)		Spare motor coaches.
4. 1932	14	14	14	14	–	–	–	(a)	7x8	MW stock – steel panelled.
	–	–	–	5	–	–	–	(b)		Used to lengthen 5x7 MW stock in 3(a) above to 5x8 MW stock.
	4	–	–	–	–	–	–	(c)	2x7	VT stock using Saloon trailers.
5. 1935	–	–	–	–	–	–	3			Converted to lengthen 3x7 MV stock in '2' above and to become 3x8 MW stock.
6. 1935–40	–	–	–	–	–	–	–			All motor cars increased from 5 to 6 compartments with stock formed 15x8 MW (30 motors and 90 CT/T), giving 30 spare motors cars (see note * below).
7. 1940	–	–	–	–	2	4	1			Start of conversion of MW stock and Dreadnought coaches to e.p. brakes. Programme halted after one train completed. Stock then revised to 8x8T and 10x6T (38 motors, 94 CT/T, giving 22 spare motor coaches and 3 spare (CT/T).
Totals:	**60**	**24**	**24**	**24**	**8**	**10**	**7**			

Grand Total: 157 cars

Note * The 30 spare motor coaches became available from –

6 in 3x8 W stock in (1) 12 in 6x7/8 VT stock in (3c) 4 in 2x7 VT stock in 4(c).
4 in 2x8 W stock in (3b) 4 spare in (3d)

The requirement for T stock in service on the Watford/Rickmansworth line changed very little during the post-war years and can be summarised as follows from 1942: In May 1942 the stock requirement was 15x8 MW and 1x8 W stock, but by 2 November 1942 the same number of trains (16) was identified as being 8x8T, 7x6T and 1x8 W stock. The total of 16 trains remained almost constant until near their end with only slight variations to compositions. From 3 May 1943 it was 9x8T and 7x6T, changed to 8x8T and 8x6T from 4 October 1943. This continued to hold good, apart from a 'blip' in 1945 when the T stock required was slightly reduced to 8x8T and 7x6T – normality (8x8T and 8x6T) was restored from 1 October of that year.

Although there was such a large number of spare motor coaches, all were kept operational. The number of casualties was very small and apart from 2707 and 2752 described above, plus 2743 and 2740 scrapped in 1950 and 1951 respectively, the fleet continued to remain intact.

An all-steel 1933 DM of T stock passing Neasden in June 1952. These cars were much more plain than previous batches, having no mouldings. *Peter Hay*

The driving ends of two T stock control trailers face each other at Watford. No.6718 on the left was built in 1930 as a proper control trailer, whilst 6709 on the right was converted in 1929 from a nine-compartment Dreadnought steam stock coach. The give-away in the latter is that the equipment was installed in the end compartment, which retained its end compartment windows. *David Hibbert*

DRIVING MOTOR COACHES – 60

Orig. No.	LT No.	Date	Built	Disposal	Orig. No.	LT No.	Date	Built	Disposal
200	2700	1927	MCW	06.04.59	230	2730	1930	BRCW	
201	2701	1927	MCW		231	2731	1930	BRCW	
202	2702	1927	MCW		232	2732	1930	BRCW	
203	2703	1927	MCW		233	2733	1930	BRCW	
204	2704	1927	MCW		234	2734	1930	BRCW	
205	2705	1927	MCW		235	2735	1930	BRCW	
206	2706	1927	MCW		236	2736	1930	BRCW	
207	2707	1927	MCW‡		237	2737	1930	BRCW	
208	2708	1927	MCW		238	2738	1930	BRCW	
209	2709	1927	MCW		239	2739	1930	BRCW	
210	2710	1927	MCW		240	2740	1930	BRCW	18.06.51
211	2711	1927	MCW		241	2741	1930	BRCW	
212	2712	1930	BRCW		242	2742*	1932	BRCW	
213	2713	1930	BRCW	06.04.59	243	2743*	1932	BRCW	20.09.50
214	2714	1930	BRCW	06.04.59	244	2744*	1932	BRCW	
215	2715	1930	BRCW		245	2745*	1932	BRCW	06.04.59
216	2716	1930	BRCW		246	2746*	1932	BRCW	
217	2717	1930	BRCW		247	2747*	1932	BRCW	
218	2718	1930	BRCW		248	2748*	1932	BRCW	
219	2719	1930	BRCW		249	2749*	1932	BRCW	
220	2720	1930	BRCW		250	2750*	1932	BRCW	
221	2721	1930	BRCW		251	2751*	1932	BRCW	
222	2722	1930	BRCW		252	2752*	1932	BRCW‡	
223	2723	1930	BRCW		253	2753*	1932	BRCW	
224	2724	1930	BRCW		254	2754*	1932	BRCW	
225	2725	1930	BRCW		255	2755*	1932	BRCW	
226	2726	1930	BRCW		256	2756*	1932	BRCW	
227	2727	1930	BRCW		257	2757*	1932	BRCW	
228	2728	1930	BRCW		258	2758*	1932	BRCW	
229	2729	1930	BRCW		259	2759*	1932	BRCW	

* Steel-panelled motor cars.
‡ Converted to experimental trailers (see pages 111–113)

DRIVING TRAILERS – 32

Orig. No.	LT No.	Date	Built	Orig. No.	LT No.	Date	Built
477	6706*	1920	MAR	536	6722†	1932	BRCW
478	6707*	1920	MAR	537	6723†	1932	BRCW
479	6708*	1920	MAR	538	6724†	1932	BRCW
480	6709*	1920	MAR	539	6725†	1932	BRCW
481	6710*	1920	MAR	540	6726†	1932	BRCW
482	6711*	1920	MAR	541	6727†	1932	BRCW
526	6712	1930	BRCW	542	6728†	1932	BRCW
527	6713	1930	BRCW	543	6729†	1932	BRCW
528	6714	1930	BRCW	544	6730†	1932	BRCW
529	6715	1930	BRCW	545	6731†	1932	BRCW
530	6716	1930	BRCW	546	6732†	1932	BRCW
531	6717	1930	BRCW	547	6733†	1932	BRCW
532	6718	1930	BRCW	548	6734†	1932	BRCW
533	6719	1930	BRCW	549	6735†	1932	BRCW
534	6720	1930	BRCW	484	6743‡	1920	MAR
535	6721	1930	BRCW	487	6746‡	1920	MAR

* Converted ex-steam stock in 1929.
‡ Converted ex-steam stock in 1940.
† Steel-panelled driving trailers.

FIRST CLASS TRAILERS (7-COMPARTMENT) – 34

Orig. No.	LT No.	Date	Built	Orig. No.	LT No.	Date	Built
460	9716*	1920	MAR	570	9733†	1932	BRCW
461	9717*	1920	MAR	571	9734†	1932	BRCW
462	9718*	1920	MAR	572	9735†	1932	BRCW
505	9719*	1923	MAR	573	9736†	1932	BRCW
506	9720*	1923	MAR	574	9737†	1932	BRCW
507	9721*	1923	MAR	575	9738†	1932	BRCW
511	9722	1930	BRCW	576	9739†	1932	BRCW
512	9723	1930	BRCW	577	9740†	1932	BRCW
513	9724	1930	BRCW	578	9741†	1932	BRCW
514	9725	1930	BRCW	579	9742†	1932	BRCW
515	9726	1930	BRCW	580	9743†	1932	BRCW
516	9727	1930	BRCW	581	9744†	1932	BRCW
517	9728	1930	BRCW	582	9745†	1932	BRCW
518	9729	1930	BRCW	449	9812‡	1920	MAR
519	9730	1930	BRCW	455	9818‡	1920	MAR
520	9731	1930	BRCW	457	9820‡	1920	MAR
569	9732†	1932	BRCW	458	9821‡	1920	MAR

* Converted ex-steam stock in 1929.
‡ Converted ex-steam stock in 1940.
† Steel-panelled trailers.

THIRD CLASS TRAILERS (9-COMPARTMENT) – 31

Orig. No.	LT No.	Date	Built	Orig. No.	LT No.	Date	Built
476	9773*	1920	MAR	558	9789†	1932	BRCW
500	9774*	1923	MAR	559	9790†	1932	BRCW
501	9775*	1923	MAR	560	9791†	1932	BRCW
521	9776	1930	BRCW	561	9792†	1932	BRCW
522	9777	1930	BRCW	562	9793†	1932	BRCW
523	9778	1930	BRCW	563	9794†	1932	BRCW
524	9779	1930	BRCW	564	9795†	1932	BRCW
525	9780	1930	BRCW	565	9796†	1932	BRCW
550	9781#	1932	BRCW	566	9797†	1932	BRCW
551	9782#	1932	BRCW	567	9798†	1932	BRCW
552	9783#	1932	BRCW	568	9799†	1932	BRCW
553	9784#	1932	BRCW	497	9800§	1923	MAR
554	9785#	1932	BRCW	498	9801§	1923	MAR
555	9786†	1932	BRCW	499	9802§	1923	MAR
556	9787†	1932	BRCW	504	9842‡	1923	MAR
557	9788†	1932	BRCW				

* Converted ex-steam stock in 1929.
§ Converted ex-steam stock in 1935.
‡ Converted ex-steam stock in 1940.
† Steel-panelled trailers.
# Steel-panelled trailers but fitted with 'mouldings' to match earlier cars.

The two experimental Metropolitan Line trailers were built on the underframes of withdrawn T stock motor cars. Nearest the camera of the two is 17001. *H. Clarke/LURS*

EXPERIMENTAL METROPOLITAN TRAILERS

The 1935 New Works Programme as planned affected the complete Underground network in some way, to a greater or lesser extent. Much work was done prior to the outbreak of the Second World War, but much was also still at the preparatory stage. After the end of hostilities, some of the outstanding work was completed, some of it was abandoned all together, while some was put on hold for completion in the future. Some of the plans for the Metropolitan Line fell into the last category, being the four tracking north of Harrow-on-the-Hill to Rickmansworth and electrification beyond. Initial proposals were to use EMU compartment T Stock and plans were drawn up to implement such a scheme. However, wartime conditions saw the plans 'put on ice'.

Many proposals were put forward as to what the rolling stock on the Metropolitan 'main line' might be, when work resumed after the war.

These included:

- Express EMUs incorporating a buffet car.
- Diesel electric locomotives or 'tenders' to work trains north of Rickmansworth.
- Compartment type stock with air-operated sliding doors, for which mock-ups were built at Acton Works in 1939.

While mindful of the fact that the passengers of the Metropolitan 'main line' preferred compartment trains to open saloon cars, LT was more concerned with the safety aspect of operating such trains in tunnel sections without through access between cars and the possibility of swing doors opening outwards in the tunnel. This effectively spelt the end for any new compartment stock on the Underground, and when work resumed on the project in 1944, the options were centred around saloon accommodation. To that end, therefore, two trial trailer cars were built at Acton Works using the underframes of two motor coaches – it should be remembered that T stock motor coaches were plentiful. The bodies of 2707 and 2752 were recorded as being scrapped on 1 November 1944.

A number of mock-ups were thus built, trying to incorporate and combine the compartment stock layout with air-operated sliding doors. The end result was two cars of saloon type running in service prior to any new replacement stock being built in bulk.

The first car, numbered 17000 (ex–2752), made its debut in 1946 and was officially recorded by London Transport as entering service on 28 January. The interior seating layout was as unique as it was revolutionary. With most of the seats being in the centre of the car in back-to-back groups of three, on one side a continuous gangway was provided, while the other side was divided into three sections with the dividing (or 'partition') seats (which had space for four passengers) extending to the body side. There was accommodation for 57 seated passengers in 'shaped' seats, while other features included fluorescent lighting, luggage racks (over the seating areas) and passenger open/close door push buttons.

The second car, ex–2707, was numbered 20000 and entered service in June 1947. It was far more luxurious than 17000. In common with other 'saloon' stock types, it retained the traditional centre gangway arrangement with pairs of individually shaped seats on each side of the gangway. Seating 56, it too had fluorescent lighting and passenger door control push buttons, but one pair of double doors on each side had a centre pillar – a feature that was provided on air-door tube stock up to 1928.

Although both cars were totally different in both interior and exterior appearance, they were both finished in London Transport red livery. They were, however, formed up in a train of T stock, and to operate the air doors, control trailer 6727 was suitably modified with the necessary equipment, although the train had to carry an additional guard to operate the air-door equipment. Trailer 17000 was not at all liked by the majority, with its unusual layout and seating arrangement, and was withdrawn for further interior modifications at Acton Works on 25 May 1949. It re-entered service on the Metropolitan Line on 2 November 1949 in modified form, but renumbered 17001. In its new guise, its interior very much formed the basis of what became the A60 stock – it was favoured above the more sumptuous car 20000. Car 17001 had all transverse seats arranged in the 3+2 layout. Some seats were provided with high back, others with lower backs. With the evaluation trials at an end (and to save the cost of an extra guard on the train), the cars were withdrawn in 1953 and are recorded as being scrapped on 25 May 1955.

EXPERIMENTAL SALOON TRAILER CONVERSIONS – 2

T Stock No.	Reno.	Date	Reno.	Date	Disposal
2752	17000	28.01.46	**17001**	02.11.49	25.05.55
2707	**20000**	11.06.47			25.05.55

Opposite top Interior of experimental saloon trailer 17001, which had been built on the underframe of a former T stock motor car, showing the different height seat backs. *Bob Greenaway collection*

Opposite lower Interior of the more luxurious trailer 20000 showing the individual pairs of seats. *LT Museum*

CHAPTER TEN

LOCOMOTIVES

STEAM LOCOMOTIVES

The vast majority of Underground services in 1933 were EMU operated. However, there remained the outer suburban services on the Metropolitan Line that were steam-hauled. This included the 'main line', where services were steam-hauled north of Rickmansworth to Aylesbury and Verney Junction, and the Brill branch shuttle to and from Quainton Road.

Not surprisingly the sleepy Brill branch was soon closed by London Transport, the last day of operation being 30 November 1935. The section between Aylesbury and Verney Junction closed to Metropolitan service on 4 July 1936, although the Metropolitan did provide a limited service between Aylesbury and Quainton Road between May 1943 and May 1948.

The story of the Metropolitan's steam locomotives is quite detailed, but because London Transport steam passenger services north of Rickmansworth were handed over to the LNER from 1 November 1937, our period of review is thus necessarily brief. At that time, some Metropolitan steam locomotives passed to LNER ownership whilst others were transferred to departmental stock for freight and engineering duties. The locomotives can be summarised as follows:

CLASS 'A' – 4–4–0T

Five locomotives of 1866–1870 vintage built for the Metropolitan Railway by Beyer Peacock survived into LT ownership in 1933, comprising Nos. 23 (built 1866), 27 (1868), 41 (1869), 48 and 49 (both 1870). There were originally 44 in the class, along with 22 of similar 'B' class and 54 for the Metropolitan District Railway.

The only passenger service worked by the surviving locomotives was on the Brill branch. It was perhaps not surprising that with its closure in 1935 that No. 27 was scrapped in that year, followed by 41, 48 and 49 in 1936. No. 23 was retained for departmental uses and was renumbered L45 in 1937. It was finally withdrawn on 3 June 1948 and was retained for preservation.

One of the five remaining Beyer Peacock 4–4–0T locomotives which survived when the LPTB came into being in July 1933. No.49 stands at Quainton Road whilst working on the Brill branch service.
LCGB/Ken Nunn Collection

The Metropolitan's furthest outpost on 'main line' services was at Verney Junction, where a train awaits departure in 1935 with an H class 4–4–4T locomotive leading a rake of Dreadnought coaches. *Photomatic*

CLASS 'E' – 0–4–4T

Seven 0–4–4T locomotives were built at Neasden Works (Nos. 77–78 in 1896 and No. 1 in 1898) and Hawthorn Leslie in 1900 (Nos. 79–80) and 1901 (Nos. 81–82). They were effectively replaced on passenger train duties by the advent of the 'H' class (q.v. below) in 1920–21, but still made occasional appearances on such workings. Nos. 78, 79 and 82 were scrapped in 1935 but Nos. 1, 77, 80 and 81 were renumbered L44, L46, L47 and L48 respectively in 1937, when they were absorbed into the departmental fleet. Even after 1937, however, it was still possible for them to work on occasional passenger services north of Rickmansworth should an LNER locomotive not be available.

CLASS 'H' – 4–4–4T

Built specifically for passenger working in 1920–21, eight locomotives were built by Kerr Stuart and were numbered 103–110. They enabled improved services to be provided, being more powerful than their predecessors. With the transfer of steam passenger services to the LNER in 1937, these locomotives were sold to them and survived with their new owners until 1942–1947.

Mention should also be made of two other classes of locomotives. These were the 'G' class 0–6–4T of which four were built in 1915 by the Yorkshire Engineering Co. and were numbered 94–97, along with the 'K' class 2–6–4T built in 1925 by Armstrong Whitworth & Co., comprising six locomotives numbered 111–116. Both G and K classes were built for freight working but did find occasional use on passenger duties. Like the 'H' class, both the G and K classes were sold to the LNER in 1937, surviving until 1943–1948.

A pair of District Railway electric locomotives are seen after leaving Ealing Broadway, on one of the District Line's Southend through services. Along with the service, these were withdrawn in 1939 and scrapped soon after. *Author's collection*

DISTRICT ELECTRIC LOCOMOTIVES

The District Railway ordered ten electric locomotives as part of its electrification scheme for 1905. These were to work the L&NWR Outer Circle service, which originated from Broad Street, between Earl's Court and Mansion House. They began working on that service on 4 December 1905.

The ten locomotives, numbered 1A to 10A, were built by Metropolitan Amalgamated. They were just over 25ft long, and although much shorter, they were similar in front-end appearance to the 1905 B stock, having the same front end design, with the clerestory roof tapering down at each end to a horizontal roof line. Driver's controls were fitted at one end only.

Because the District Railway required its tracks east of Earl's Court for its own service improvements, the Outer Circle service was terminated at Earl's Court from 1 January 1909, rendering the ten locomotives surplus to requirements. For a short period of time, they found use top and tailing four-car trains of B stock trailers on the Inner Circle, this service then being jointly operated by the District and the Metropolitan. However, negotiations were already underway with the London, Tilbury & Southend Railway to provide a limited through service from Ealing Broadway to Southend, which began on 1 June 1910. Shoeburyness was reached by this service the following year. The coaching stock was provided by the LT&SR and pairs of District electric locomotives hauled them between Ealing Broadway and Barking, from where LT&S steam locomotives continued. Three locomotives, 1A, 9A and 10A, were still regarded as surplus and were scrapped in 1911, the remaining seven being adequate for the through service. To maintain number continuity, locomotive 8A, then the last of the group, was renumbered 1A. Later, the 'A' suffix was dropped and they were subsequently given an 'L' prefix.

The locomotives were renovated at the then new Acton Works in the 1920s, receiving surplus GE260 equipment from the too powerful F stock motor cars. Four locomotives were also converted to double-ended status (1A, 3A, 4A and 7A), while 2A remained single-ended facing west, and 5A and 6A single-ended facing east.

Two locomotives were prematurely withdrawn in 1938 and scrapped, while the remaining five soldiered on. The outbreak of the Second World War resulted in the through Ealing – Southend service being withdrawn on 30 September 1939 and the five remaining locomotives were scrapped soon afterwards. The equipment from these locomotives in fact returned to whence they came – as part of the improvements being made to the F stock fleet, 12 control trailers were undergoing conversion to single-equipped motor cars, and the equipment from the locomotives was used for this purpose.

Under a unified LPTB, it was proposed to use spare Metropolitan electric locomotives on the Ealing – Southend service and contemporary reports suggest that some trials may have taken place to that end. However, there is no evidence to suggest that this did happen, although it is known that crew training was being planned just before the service was withdrawn. After hostilities had ceased in 1945, this particular Underground service was never reinstated.

METROPOLITAN ELECTRIC LOCOMOTIVES

The 20 electric locomotives inherited by the new LPTB in 1933 were built in 1922–23 and replaced 20 locomotives that were built by Metropolitan Amalgamated with British Westinghouse equipment in 1905 (Nos.1–10) and with BTH equipment in 1907 (Nos.11–20). Both batches of locomotives were 'double-ended', in that they could be driven in either direction, but the first batch were 'camel-back' locomotives which had a double set of controls in a central cab with the equipment either side, sloping downwards to the fronts. The second batch of locomotives had flat-fronted ends with controls at each end, with the equipment located down each side.

Improvements to rolling stock and services were planned by the Metropolitan Railway in 1919 and this included re-equipping and reconstructing all 20 locomotives to make them more powerful. No.17 was the first selected and was completed in 1921. It was different in appearance to the two previous types, the cab ends being 'V'-shaped. This set the general design for the other 19 locomotives although by this stage, rebuilding had been abandoned in favour of new locomotives – No.17 was later altered to match the others. The contract for the new locomotives was awarded to Vickers Ltd. of Barrow-in-Furness, who was the successor to British Westinghouse. The equipment was mounted in the centre section of the locomotives, with gangway access on both sides. Driving controls were provided at each end. They were delivered in 1922–23 and took the same number series (1–20).

It was decided in March 1927 that the locomotives should be named, mostly to recognise celebrities in the areas of Metroland that the locomotives would be working. There were several changes to plans in allocating the names, the final allocation being as follows:

1.	John Lyon	11.	George Romney
2.	Oliver Cromwell	12.	Sarah Siddons
3.	Sir Ralph Verney	13.	Dick Whittington
4.	Lord Byron	14.	Benjamin Disraeli
5.	John Hampden	15.	Wembley 1924
6.	William Penn	16.	Oliver Goldsmith
7.	Edmund Burke	17.	Florence Nightingale
8.	Sherlock Holmes	18.	Michael Faraday
9.	John Milton	19.	John Wycliffe
10.	William Ewart Gladstone	20.	Sir Christopher Wren

The 'odd-man-out' in the naming was locomotive No.15, which commemorated its exhibition at the British Empire Exhibition at Wembley in 1925. The first locomotive to receive its name plates was No.17 on 3 October 1927 and others gradually followed suit.

When the LPTB took over the Metropolitan's rolling stock in 1933, the first locomotive to be overhauled was No.19, which was finished with elaborate lining out. Others subsequently followed. The Second World War resulted in the service stock grey livery being applied to the locomotives from 1942. From the following year, the bronze nameplates began to be removed. This was not such a simple task, as it involved removing and replacing the side panels and was not complete until 1948, three years after the war ended! In reality, however, there was a genuine reluctance to remove them as indicated by the speed in which it was done – a 'patch' over the side panels would have sufficed.

In Metropolitan Railway livery, electric locomotive No.1 'John Lyon' is in Neasden depot on 11 March 1933, shortly before it was to pass into LT ownership.
H.C. Casserley

Seen at Rickmansworth on 10 September 1946 is No.16 'Oliver Goldsmith'. Such was the lack of enthusiasm for removing the names from the locomotives during the Second World War, that this locomotive still has them on, well over a year after the war had finished. The locomotive has just come off one of the few through services to Quainton Road, which were restored on a temporary basis between 1943 and 1948.
H.C. Casserley